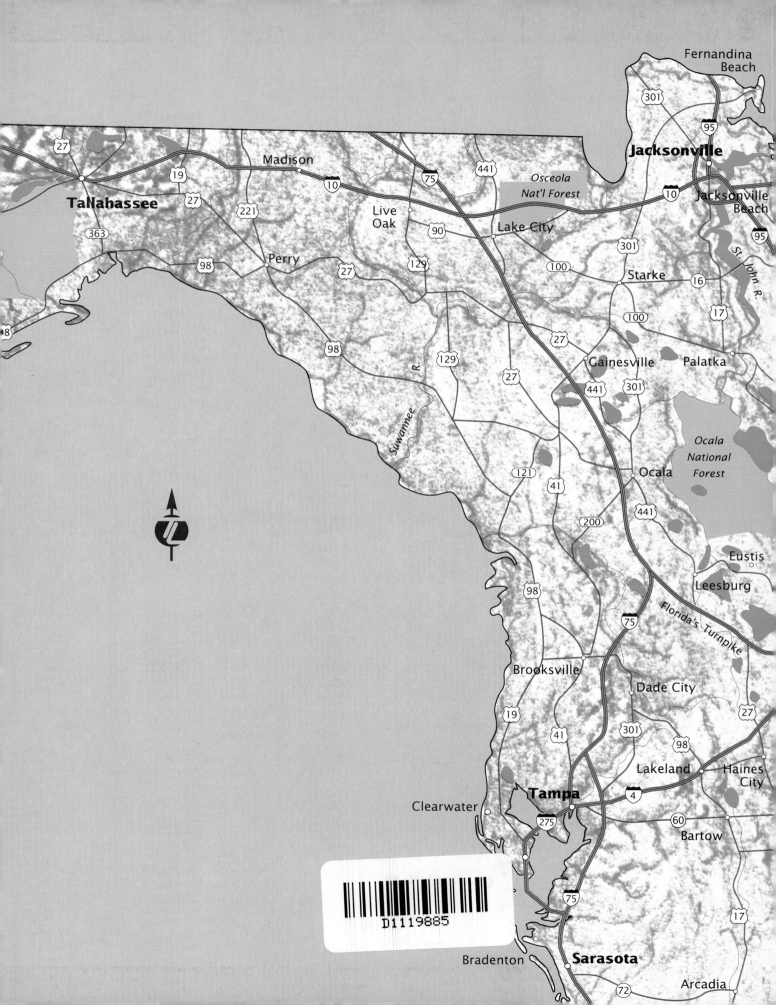

OTHER BOOKS BY TRAILER LIFE

RVing America's Backroads:

Diana and Bill Gleasner

…Light-hearted I take to the open road,
Healthy, free, the world before me,
The long brown path before me leading
wherever I choose."

Walt Whitman, *Song of the Open Road*

Trailer Life Books
Agoura, California

DEDICATION
To Stephen and Suzanne Gleasner
Good Friends on the Road Less Traveled

Trailer Life Book Division

President: Richard Rouse
Vice President/General Manager: Ted Binder
Vice President/Publisher, Book Division: Michael Schneider
General Manager, Book Division: Rena Copperman
Assistant Manager, Book Division: Cindy Lang

Cover design: Bob Schroeder
Cover photograph: Bill Gleasner
Interior design: David Fuller/Robert S. Tinnon
Color Consultant: Mirante Almazan
Production manager: Rena Copperman
Editorial assistant: Judi Lazarus
Indexer: Barbara Wurf
Maps: EarthSurface Graphics

All photographs are the authors' unless otherwise credited.

This book was set in ITC Garamond Book by Andresen's Tucson
Typographics and printed on 60-pound Consoweb Brilliant by
R.R. Donnelley and Sons in Willard, Ohio.

ISBN 0-934798-22-2

Library of Congress Cataloging-in-Publication Data

Gleasner, Diana C.
    RVing America's backroads: Florida.

    Includes index.
    1. Automobiles—Florida—Touring.   2. Recreational vehicles—
Florida.   3. Florida—Description and travel—1981–   —Guide-
books.   I. Gleasner, Bill.   II. Title.
GV1024.G56   1989   91759   88-24800
ISBN 0-934798-22-2

Contents

ACKNOWLEDGMENTS

We don't know how anyone can write a book on Florida without the help of Greg Yon at the Florida Division of Tourism. He knows everyone in Florida and is a veritable geyser of information. In fact, all the folks we talked to at the Division of Tourism are a credit to their profession.

Our research for this book was launched with the able assistance of Joice Veselka, a real pro who is as generous as she is competent. Bill Hensley, who has been a staunch ally over the years, was once again right there when we needed him. Bob Scott, problem solver of the first order, cleared the way for an extremely satisfying day photographing at Red Coconut RV Park. RVers Ed and Susan Cottle and Joanne and John Storch provided some excellent suggestions, and our Hawaiian cat, who has been remarkably philosophical about our absences, faithfully guarded the premises.

The following Floridians shared their enthusiasm and expertise with us: Janette Hunt, Gary Stogner, Lee Daniel, Raymond Singer, Pat Tolle, Stuart and Andy Newman, Charles Ridgway, Ken Carden, Margaret Goff Clark, and Jonellen Heckler.

From the very first chat with our editor, Rena Copperman of T.L. Enterprises, we knew our relationship would be a pleasant one. Her unflappable cheerfulness, excellent judgment, constant encouragement, keen sense of humor, and steady hand on the helm have been greatly appreciated. Thanks, Rena.

We always roll into Florida with memories in high gear, ghosts of trips past entangling us like a web of tropical vines. Our flashbacks are of sunny, exuberantly happy times—swimming with the dolphins in the Keys, riding horseback on Amelia Island, Mickey Mouse kissing our beaming daughter, our son landing his first sea trout in the Everglades. Memories never fail to rev up our expectations. We have not yet been disappointed.

The thousands of miles we covered while researching and photographing this book confirmed what we already knew—RVing is the ideal way to absorb Florida's incredible natural beauty firsthand. Whether tucked into the tranquil dunes of St. Joseph Peninsula, watching the moonrise from John Pennekamp Coral Reef State Park, or feeding gulls on Estero Beach, we enjoyed the serendipitous pleasures of the RV life as fully as our planned activities.

We hope it will be the same for you. The secret is to take time to savor your surroundings. Pull off the major highways, poke along the state's backroads, and open yourself to the riches of Florida's less-heralded attractions. For beyond the crowded attractions and condo-lined beaches, the modern-day explorer will find discoveries to last a lifetime.

During the summer months, reservations may be advisable at certain attractions, and a call in advance may save hours of frustration in waiting, or prevent the disappointment of being turned away. It's especially important to note that many attractions offer discounts that may be best arranged for by calling ahead. An example is the Golden Eagle Passport offered by the federal government. It presently costs $25 a year and can be obtained in person or by mail from the National Park Service, U.S. Department of the Interior, 18th and C streets, N.W., Washington, D.C. 20240. The Golden Age Passport is free to permanent U.S. residents who are 62 or older; the Golden Access Passport is free to permanently blind or disabled travelers. These latter two must be applied for in person at most federally operated recreation areas that charge an entrance fee.

Finally, bear in mind that while every attempt has been made to assure that information on routes, road conditions, entrance fees, and other factual matter was accurate at press time, inevitably things change. Therefore, as you retrace our route and follow in our footsteps we urge you to draw upon these same sources to supplement this guide.

FLORIDA

Florida was made for the RVer. Consider its terrific state park system, two national parks, and a multitude of private campgrounds that range from posh to homey. Think of splendid scenery, friendly people, incredibly rich history (this is where colonization of the country started), and out-of-the-way gems that seem to delight at every turn in the road. Then never mind all that. Just think of the magnificent weather.

This subtropical Eden fascinates foreigners and Americans alike. Perhaps it is because our most primordial human instincts are stirred by its promises of warm seas and lush landscapes. Florida's siren call has become an indelible part of our national psyche. Just knowing this slender sunbaked peninsula exists is somehow a comfort.

But few realize the astonishing diversity offered by this state. They know that Walt Disney World is the home of Mickey Mouse, but most have never laid eyes on one of Florida's shyest residents, the manatee. The media has covered the annual migration of college students but missed the bird rookeries in the Ten Thousand Islands that are just as noisy, crowded, and teeming with life as Fort Lauderdale beaches in the spring. Everyone is aware of the high-rise glitter of Miami Beach, but how many have explored the Dry Tortugas?

As visitors to EPCOT Center's Future World learn about the computers of tomorrow, an Everglades alligator stalks its prey with time-honored efficiency. While race cars set speed records at Daytona, a mastodon skeleton slumbers in the valley of the Peace River. Astronauts may blast off to the moon, but Seminole Indians still prepare for their annual Green Corn Dance just as their ancestors did.

Four thousand of Florida's 58,000 square miles are water. The land is spackled with countless springs (Wakulla claims to be the world's deepest at 185 feet) and 30,000 lakes, including Lake Okeechobee, the second largest natural body of fresh water wholly within the United States.

The northern section of the state features rolling, red clay hills, pine forests, Spanish moss, and a rare newsworthy snow. The myriad lakes and palm trees of central Florida gradually give way to the prairies of sawgrass and mangrove swamps of the Everglades. Nearly tropical, the Keys enjoy summer weather year round.

It is the promise of sunshine that first attracts visitors. Like Ponce de León searching for the fountain of eternal youth, they come in droves to see if this fabled land basking in the sunshine can possibly be real. They return again and again when they find it is.

THE HIGH ROAD
From Pensacola to Tallahassee

Everybody needs beauty as well as bread, places to play in and pray in, where Nature may heal and cheer and give strength to body and soul alike.

John Muir

If you take the high road (the northern route) from Pensacola to Tallahassee, you will find a Florida few folks are familiar with. We couldn't decide if the scenery looked more like Maine, Canada, or the foothills of Virginia.

Someone could design an entire Trivial Pursuit game around this tour. Where can you find fall color, one of only two perfectly round lakes in the world, stalactites and stalagmites, or Florida's only waterfalls?

Pensacola

It seemed logical to start at the beginning, and Pensacola, the westernmost city in Florida, is where it all began. Before Captain John Smith, long before the pilgrims, even six years before the founding of St. Augustine, settlers arrived on these shores planning to make their homes on this strange wild continent.

In 1559 Spanish conquistador Tristan de Luna landed with 500 soldiers, 1,000 colonists, and very high hopes. Santa Maria, the name he gave the new community, wasn't the ideal place to be, but the group was grimly determined. After two years a hurricane shattered the settlement, bringing its struggles to a decisive end.

The Spanish built Fort San Carlos in 1698, but ultimately it would take five attempts and nearly 200 years to establish a permanent settlement. The seaport's location made it a prime target for attack, and it had great strategic military importance. During its stormy history, the community lived under five flags and through seventeen changes of government. Spain, Great Britain, France, the United States, and the Confederacy fought for control with the result that there were more battles for the possession of Pensacola than for any other location in the United States.

When Spain finally decided to sell Florida to the United States in 1821, Andrew Jackson, who had already led two invasions of the city, came to Pensacola to complete the transaction. This was the capital of the state until 1822, and Jackson lived here as the first territorial governor of Florida. Both he and Mrs. Jackson were miserable in a place that they described as "filthy" and "heathen."

They would not recognize the city today. Pensacola survived more than four centuries of upheaval, including Indian raids, wars, fires, hurricanes, and yellow fever epidemics to emerge in its present form. We learned a good deal about these trials and tribulations at the Pensacola Historical Museum and the West Florida Museum of History.

Preservation of the past is an ongoing process, as we discovered driving by some of the gingerbread Victorian homes in the North Hill Preserva-

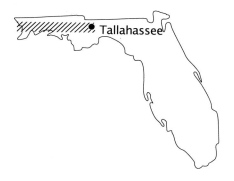

Tour 1 244 miles

PENSACOLA • BIG LAGOON STATE RECREATION AREA • BLACKWATER RIVER STATE PARK • DE FUNIAK SPRINGS • FALLING WATERS STATE RECREATION AREA • FLORIDA CAVERNS STATE PARK • TORREYA STATE PARK • LAKE JACKSON MOUNDS STATE ARCHAEOLOGICAL SITE • MACLAY GARDENS

After Florida left the Union in 1861 nearly all federal property in the state was seized by Secessionists, but a notable exception occurred at Pensacola. Rebel troops were never able to take Fort Pickens, but they did take control of all other installations in the area. In a November, 1861, battle, Fort Barrancas had its flagstaff shot away and its walls slightly scarred, but casualties were light due to the strong walls. That combat turned out to be the last for the fort. In May, 1862, the Confederates pulled out of Pensacola, and Union forces reoccupied all the harbor installations.

De Funiak's Glory Days.
During the 1880s an enterprising railroad executive declared, "The railroad must come by this beautiful lake [Lake De Funiak], and we must make this a splendid winter resort," and for forty years (beginning in 1885) the community hosted a program of concerts and educational lectures known as the Florida Chautauqua. A Chautauqua Festival held here each spring commemorates this era, which was brought to an end by the Great Depression.

Sunset View.
Visitors can enjoy a sunset view of the Intracoastal Waterway and Gulf Islands National Seashore from Big Lagoon State Recreation Area, ten miles southwest of Pensacola.

tion District and exploring the Seville Square area on foot. Maps of these sections and other information are available at the Visitor Information Center (on the Pensacola side of the bridge), which has thoughtfully provided a separate parking area for RVs.

Camping at Big Lagoon

We camped in the Big Lagoon State Recreation Area about ten miles southwest of Pensacola off State Road (SR) 292. Besides proximity to town, it offers fine facilities and an abundance of natural beauty. An extensive boardwalk system enabled us to observe shore birds feeding in the salt marsh, and we enjoyed watching boat traffic on the Intracoastal Waterway from the observation tower in the East Beach area.

The U.S. Naval Aviation Museum

How could we pass up the United States Naval Aviation Museum? The only museum in the world devoted to naval aviation, it is practically around the corner, and what's more, it's free. We were absolutely intrigued by this sprawling two-story complex with its handsome displays. From balloons with wicker gondolas and a gallery of large oil paintings to a whole ballpark of historic aircraft, this museum is first class all the way.

We tried the controls of a jet trainer and watched movies in several different small theaters. The most inspiring film, *The Great Flight*, told the dramatic story of the first successful crossing of the Atlantic Ocean by air in 1919.

On a more contemporary note is the Skylab Command Module with its Space Age drama. The nation's first space station, launched on May 14, 1973, suffered extensive damage within sixty-three seconds of lift-off. The Skylab Command Module, scheduled to launch the following day, was delayed more than a week as NASA engineers worked around the clock to improvise tools and materials for the Skylab's repair. After a 7½-hour chase through space, the astronauts were able to link up, repair the crippled laboratory, and continue their experiments. They rode the command module back to earth twenty-eight days later. The module was loaned to the Naval Aviation Museum by the Smithsonian Institution.

While we were in the neighborhood, we crossed the road to look around Fort Barrancas. On the site of seventeenth-century Spanish fortifications, Barrancas and its attached Water Battery have been faithfully restored according to old documents in the National Archives. "We're part of Gulf Islands National Seashore," the ranger explained, "but most folks don't know we're here. Some of them stumble on us when they visit the Naval Aviation Museum." We didn't admit that we, too, were stumblers who noticed signs to the fort as we were leaving the museum.

The White Sands of Blackwater River

Our April weather was warm and sunny, but we had the campground to ourselves at Blackwater River State Park. Located in Blackwater River State Forest, the park is about fifteen miles northeast of Milton. We spent a glisteny morning on the beach (well, it seemed like a beach). We've seen river sandbars before, but nothing to compare with these wide expanses of sugar-white sand at every bend. The brochure claims this is one of the cleanest rivers in the country, and, in our opinion, it is certainly one of the prettiest. We wished for time for a canoe trip from the river's source in Alabama to its end in Blackwater Bay. Next time, for sure.

Historic De Funiak Springs

Following US Highway 90, which parallels Interstate 10 (I-10), to De Funiak Springs, we found Lake De Funiak, said to be one of two perfectly round lakes in the world. The pleasant setting inspired an enterprising railroad executive to plan for a "splendid winter resort" here in the 1880s. The railroad is still here, and the town grew up around the lake, but the resort has gone with the wind.

For a while (almost forty years) the community had its moment in the sun. The Chautauqua Committee decided this would make a fine winter site for its program of concerts and lectures given each summer at Lake Chautauqua in New York. The first meetings were held in tents, and at night fires built on platforms all around the lake illuminated the area.

Naval Aircraft Display.
The United States Naval Aviation Museum, the only museum in the world devoted exclusively to naval aviation, features more than forty full-size aircraft ranging from the A-1 *Triad*, the first aircraft purchased by the Navy in 1911, to the most modern jets. The museum is located on the grounds of the Naval Air Station in Pensacola.

Blackwater Course.
The Blackwater River, which begins in Alabama, winds through Blackwater River State Park in Blackwater River State Forest. Known for its broad sugar-white sandbars and unusually clean water, the fifty-eight-mile river is a favorite haunt of canoeists, swimmers, and campers.

A small tabernacle was constructed, and the grand Chautauqua Hotel was rushed to completion in order to host such distinguished speakers as William Jennings Bryan. Thousands flocked to De Funiak Springs (many in chartered railway cars) to participate in these cultural events, but the Great Depression brought all this activity to a screeching halt.

An annual May festival revives the spirit of Florida's Winter Chautauqua, and you can still see the nineteenth-century Chautauqua Assembly Building (now used for the Walton County Chamber of Commerce), and the handsome old homes (in varying states of restoration) that surround the lake.

One of the most distinctive structures on the lakeshore is the tiny Walton-De Funiak Public Library. Opened in 1887, the one-room building (24 by 17 feet), which cost less than $600, is thought to be Florida's oldest public library still housed in its original building. We were surprised to find a fine European armor collection (with some pieces dating back to the Crusades!) scattered about the library, but then you never know what you'll uncover when you start poking around Florida's backroads.

Falling Waters State Recreation Area

Certainly waterfalls were not on our list of things we expected to see in Florida, but then we had never heard of Falling Waters State Recreation Area. We *had* heard of sinkholes. They are a fact of life in Florida, and when a car or house falls into a newly formed sink, it sometimes makes national news.

Florida's Only Waterfall.
Falling Waters Sink, a cylindrical, smooth-walled chimney 100 feet deep with a diameter of 15 feet, is in Falling Waters State Recreation Area near Chipley. Here a small stream creates a waterfall and then flows into an underground cavern at the bottom of the sink, where hand-hewn timbers of an early grist mill can still be seen. This is a classic example of one of Florida's notable geological features, the limestone sinkhole.

The problem is caused by limestone, which is often near the surface in Florida, being slowly dissolved by weak acids in rainwater. The caverns created by this action occasionally collapse, forming a sinkhole. In Falling Waters Park a stream wandered into a 100-foot sinkhole and, sure enough, fell all the way to the bottom.

It was a pretty slim stream when we were there, but the cylindrical, smooth-walled "chimney" is impressive. We followed boardwalk trails through a pristine pine forest, passing the site of the first known attempt (1919) to find oil in Florida. Needless to say, the well was unproductive, and the area is known today for its falling water.

Between each glacial advance there was a warming period when the ice floes melted. The seas rose and Florida sank from sight. During each submersion the land was blanketed with sediments of silt, sand, and shells. This rich layering of ooze, known to scientists as oolitic limestone, *is in some places more than two miles thick. The rest of the world was already ancient when Florida finally emerged from the sea approximately nineteen million years ago to rest on its limestone bed formed from the shells of billions of sea creatures.*

Stalactites or Stalagmites?
Florida Caverns State Park features an intriguing labyrinth of underground caves studded with splendid stalactites, stalagmites, and other limestone formations. First mentioned by the Spanish in 1693, the caves sheltered Indians hiding from General Andrew Jackson's forces during his expeditions into Spanish Florida in 1818.

Going Underground at Florida Caverns State Park

Our next destination offered another version of limestone eroded by water—Florida Caverns State Park. A network of underground caves shelters exquisite formations including stalactites, stalagmites, columns, and delicate hollow soda straws. Although these are on a smaller scale, the caverns rival the beauty of some of the world's most famous.

We weren't the first to duck under these low-hanging stalactites. Indians used the caves for shelter, and the Spanish mentioned them as early as 1693. Passageways are much easier to navigate today, thanks to Civilian Conservation Corps (CCC) members who enlarged them while living here during the Depression.

Rangers give excellent tours of such wonders as the Waterfall, Cathedral, and Wedding rooms. From time to time the park also offers spelunking tours of the undeveloped caves for the adventurous who don't mind spending the better part of the afternoon on their hands and knees.

Don't miss the enlightening slide show in the visitor center that explains how the caverns are formed. Imagine stalagmites that grow at the rate of an inch every hundred years or so. Forget smoke, mirrors, and other sleights of hand. This is another kind of magic, the kind that involves one mineral-laden drop of water at a time and seems to take forever. Another neat trick is performed by the Chipola River, which does a disappearing act in the park, only to reappear several hundred feet downstream.

The rangers say this is a very popular campground since the park offers such an interesting variety of things to see and do, but the rest of the world was apparently waiting for summer. We shared the campground with only three other RVs and had the delightful Blue Hole swimming area to ourselves.

Hiking the Ravines of Torreya State Park

As we traveled eastward along US 90, we began to encounter rolling hills. We detoured southward to find Torreya State Park on SR 271 just off SR 12. Had it been autumn instead of spring, we were told, we would have also been treated to a rare (for Florida) display of fall color, not that this park needs anything to enhance its beauty.

We recommend the seven-mile-loop hiking trail for a good look at the flowers and hardwoods usually associated with north Georgia's Appalachian Mountains. Naturalists say these forested bluffs and rugged ravines were left when the glaciers receded during the Ice Age. Two extremely rare trees are found here within a twenty-mile area—the Florida yew and the park's namesake, the Torreya.

An affluent cotton planter, Jason Gregory, built his home on a nearby bluff across the Apalachicola River in the mid-1850s. In 1935 his abandoned house was dismantled, floated across the river, and reassembled. No easy task, this took almost three years. Now restored to its nineteenth-century appearance, the Gregory house is open for guided tours.

We learned that life was not so simple in the "good old days" when the river was the only avenue of commerce. (This location is still remote; stock up on groceries before you reach the park.) Disease-carrying mosquitoes were vicious, and floods spelled disaster. But it was the Civil War and the abolition of slavery that brought an end to this particular plantation.

Lake Jackson Mounds

As we neared Tallahassee we were thinking of the original inhabitants of this area. The coming of the Europeans spelled doom for the Apalachee Indians who once roamed these hills and tilled the soil. When Hernando de Soto wintered here in 1539, the priests in his party celebrated what is thought to be the first Christmas mass in the New World. The conflict of the two cultures proved disastrous for the Indians, who were ousted from the land and eventually driven to extinction. The white men kept the Indian name Tallahassee, which means "old field" or "abandoned village."

Of course there were Indians here even before the Apalachees. Archaeologists have found evidence indicating the area was inhabited as early as

The Apalachicola River was an important interstate highway in the 1800s. During the great trading era, between 1840 and 1910, more than 200 steamboats plied the river.

1300 B.C. We stopped at Lake Jackson Mounds State Archaeological Site (free) to learn what we could about the early residents. The Indians who built these particular mounds were primarily farmers who raised corn, beans, and squash and traded surplus crops with nearby villages. Besides farming, they hunted deer, turkey, and turtle and gathered wild fruits and berries.

As we trudged up the wooden stairs of these tall pyramid-shaped mounds, we could think only of those early people who, without benefit of equipment, lugged one basket of clay at a time to the top. Between A.D. 1300 and A.D. 1600 this was the focal point of the best-known ceremonial center in northern Florida. In addition to the village, a burial mound and six temple mounds are located here. (Only two are on state property.) Ceremonial buildings or chiefs' houses were usually constructed on top of the mounds, and the Indians used a ramp to get to the top. Scientists can only speculate as to the exact nature of the ceremonies conducted here. Today the mounds sprout only trees, large ones at that.

After a picnic in a live oak grove, we took a half-hour ramble on the Butler Mill Trail to a grist mill site. A portion of the trail straddles the top of an earthen irrigation dike used to divert water to the surrounding fields. Apparently, humans must be born with an atavistic urge to re-arrange dirt.

Maclay Gardens

Tallahassee was founded and designated as the capital of Florida in 1824 primarily because of its location midway between Jacksonville and Pensacola. Southern enough to escape the bitter cold, the city is still far enough north to celebrate the change of seasons. The most concentrated dose of spring, we were assured, could be experienced at Maclay State Botanical Gardens.

We had just toured the plantation house at Torreya so we passed up the opportunity to see the interior of the Maclay House. Luckily, we didn't miss the gardens. They are spectacular!

This was the winter home of Alfred B. Maclay, a New York financier, who began developing his gardens in 1923. He planned the blooming season to run from January to April, with waves of color changing as spring progressed. Azaleas and camellias predominate, but more than sixty other species, including Italian cypress and oriental cherry trees, enliven the exquisite floral landscaping. Brick walkways, fountains, reflecting pools, avenues of stately palms, and a placid lake complete the picturesque scene. Maclay Gardens provided a grand finale to our northern swing through Florida's panhandle.

If you have to have endings, they might as well be beautiful. And they should also contain the seeds of new beginnings. A virulent case of spring fever was running rampant through our home on wheels. It was definitely time to roll.

POINTS OF INTEREST: Florida Tour 1

From Pensacola to Tallahassee

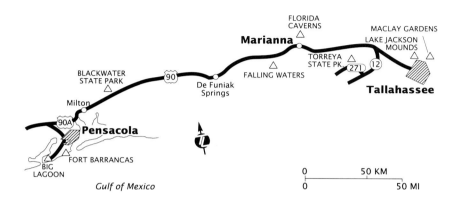

ACCESS: *US 90* south of *I-10* in Pensacola.

INFORMATION: *Tallahassee Chamber of Commerce*, 100 N. Duval Street, Box 1639, Tallahassee, FL 32302 (904) 224-8116; *Pensacola Visitors Information Center*, 1401 E. Gregory Street, Pensacola, FL 32501 (904) 434-1234; *Walton County Chamber of Commerce*, Circle Drive, P.O. Box 29, De Funiak Springs, FL 32433 (904) 892-3191; *Jackson County Chamber of Commerce*, 412 N. Jefferson Street, P.O. Box 130, Marianna, FL 32446 (904) 482-8061.

ANNUAL EVENTS:

De Funiak Springs: *Chautauqua Festival Day*, May.

Tallahassee: *Springtime Tallahassee* (home and garden tours, art shows, etc.), March/April; *North Florida Fair*, October.

Pensacola: *Blue Angel Air Show*, November; *Mardi Gras* (parades, food festival, musical events, Priscus Ball), five days prior to Ash Wednesday; *Fiesta of the Five Flags* (pageant, parades, art shows, sporting events), May.

MUSEUMS AND GALLERIES:

Pensacola: *The Naval Aviation Museum*, Naval Air Station, Pensacola, FL 32508 (904) 452-3604; *Pensacola Historical Museum*, 405 S. Adams Street at Zaragoza Street, Pensacola, FL 32501 (904) 433-1559; *West Florida Museum of History*, 200 E. Zaragoza Street, Pensacola, FL 32501 (904) 444-8905.

SPECIAL ATTRACTIONS:

Tallahassee: *Alfred B. Maclay State Gardens*, 3540 Thomasville Road, Tallahassee, FL 32308 (904) 893-4232.

Marianna: *Florida Caverns State Park*, Marianna, FL 32446 (904) 482-3632.

OUTFITTERS:

Action on Blackwater River (canoe trips), P.O. Box 283, Baker, FL 32531 (904) 537-2997.

Spelunking Tours, Florida Caverns State Park, Marianna, FL 32446 (904) 482-3632.

FLORIDA'S PANHANDLE

The Coastal Route

If there is magic on this planet, it is contained in water.

Loren Eiseley

W̲ater, water, everywhere and plenty of interesting things to do in, on, and beside it. Variations on the water theme seem to be everywhere in northwestern Florida. From salt to fresh to brackish, from the fish-crowded Gulf of Mexico to slender rivers bordered by pristine sand bars, we thought we had seen it all. Then we discovered one of the world's major springs and a strange place with the unenticing name of Dead Lakes.

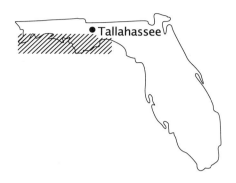

The Mysteries of Wakulla Springs

Appropriately, we began our investigation of Florida's panhandle with a visit to Wakulla Springs, one of the world's largest and deepest springs. (Wakulla is fifteen miles south of Tallahassee by way of SR 61 and SR 267.) This natural wonder, which normally produces 600,000 gallons of water per minute, outdid itself on April 11, 1973, by pumping out an astonishing 14,325 gallons per second. The remarkable spring and the lush land around it recently became Edward Ball Wakulla Springs State Park, part of Florida's state park system.

Wakulla is a Seminole Creek word variously translated as meaning "breast of life" or "mysteries of strange water." We are partial to the original Indian name for the springs—Tah-ille-ya-aha-n—which means "where the water flows upward like the rays of heavenly light out of the shadow of the hill." The Indian description is right on target.

In 1855 a journalist reported in a Jacksonville paper, "Near the spring I saw some of the remains of a mastodon that had been taken from it. The triangular bone below the knee measured 6 inches on each side." In 1935 a complete mastodon skeleton was removed from the spring.

These huge elephantlike creatures roamed the southeastern United States during the ice ages. Some scientists theorize the heavy animals fell through thin ice covering the Wakulla River. Others say hunters dragged the animals into what was then a dry cave. Whatever the real story, it seems appropriate that this was the location used for the filming of *Creature from the Black Lagoon.*

We took both boat trips offered, the jungle cruise and the glass-bottom-boat tour, and saw all manner of birds and fish. The endangered limpkin thrives here, primarily because its food—the apple snail—is abundant in the area. Often called the "crying bird," the limpkin's distinctive call has been described as sounding like "a woman lost forever in the swamps." This is one bird that has perfected extracting escargots down to a science, judging from the empty shells piled along the banks of the Wakulla.

We saw an alligator carrying several small progeny on its head, mullet jumping all over the place, and, yes, a pole-vaulting fish. Now Henry, the

Emerald Coast.
Ideal for beachcombing, jogging, or leisurely sunset strolls, this pristine stretch of sparkling sand borders the translucent green and turquoise waters of the Gulf of Mexico near Destin. The beaches of northwestern Florida, appropriately known as the Emerald Coast, are particularly dazzling because they are composed of finely ground white quartz.

Lush Life.
This baby alligator is riding high and dry at Wakulla Springs, one of the world's largest and deepest freshwater springs. These remarkable springs support a lush growth of underwater vegetation and an extraordinary abundance of wildlife. Because public access has been controlled for nearly half a century, the wildlife has remained in its primeval densities and is unwary of tour boats and their passengers.

fish, doesn't pole vault just for the fun of it. Our guide worked awfully hard to pull off this particular event.

"Henry," he called out loudly, "I want you to meet us at the pole." Well, that didn't do it. After calling again and again in a special singsong that apparently is supposed to provoke action, our guide was reduced to pleading. He tried in a more threatening tone: "Henry! Henry Junior! Henrietta!"—all to no avail. Then suddenly a fish appeared, grinned, and vaulted over the pole. Guess we'll have to chalk this one up to another of the "mysteries of strange waters."

The lodge, built in 1937 and now called Wakulla Springs Lodge and Conference Center, has a Spanish look and the air of old-time Florida. Tennessee marble floors and ceiling beams hand painted in colorful Aztec and Toltec Indian designs are clear indications this building is an original. Few franchised hotels, for instance, exhibit a former resident of the area in a Plexiglas case—"Old Joe," an alligator approximately 200 years old, weighing 650 pounds, and measuring over 11 feet long.

Wakulla Springs comes complete with a small sand beach, a diving platform, and 185 feet of water to plunge into. Nature trails lead through dense woodlands, wild turkeys scurry through the underbrush, and somewhere out there in the depths Henry is playing it very cool.

Spring Farm Days at Tallahassee Junior Museum

A woman at Wakulla Springs spoke so enthusiastically about the Tallahassee Junior Museum that we backtracked a short way (taking SR 61 north and SR 373 and SR 371 west) and spent a delightful afternoon wandering through this expansive attraction. The setting is lovely, and, quite by luck, we happened to be there in mid-April for Spring Farm Days.

We now know how to shear a sheep. You sit it on its rear haunches, get behind it, buzz right down the middle of the tummy, and it doesn't even wiggle. We listened to a weaver of tall tales, watched a woman spin wool, and a man make dye by boiling Spanish moss and water in a large iron pot over an open fire. We politely turned down an offer to scrub clothes with lye soap on an old-fashioned washboard.

The best was yet to come. Whoever designed the habitat trails did a masterful job and had a splendid area to work with, including woodlands, swamps, and lakes. As we strolled across Deer Bridge, we caught a glimpse of a doe wading between the cypress trees. These natural environments are far superior to the cages in a typical zoo setting.

Elevated walkways led us by a rare Florida panther (sleeping), black bears (yawning), foxes, raccoons, bobcats (having a tiff with each other), birds of prey (including a magnificent bald eagle that perched on a screen within arm's length), alligators, and a couple of "type-A" river otters. Although native to this area, most of the animals had been orphaned or injured and could not have survived in the wild. This excellent "museum" gave us a good look at the Florida of yesteryear, as close as some of us will ever get.

The Good Old Days.
A costumed farm wife cheerfully scrubs the family laundry on a working 1880 farm. This authentic re-creation of Florida pioneer life takes place every year during Tallahassee Junior Museum's Spring Farm Days.

Swamp Sentinel.
A white-tailed deer stands alert in a cypress swamp at the edge of Lake Bradford on the grounds of the Tallahassee Junior Museum. A network of habitat trails at this fifty-two-acre center provides a fascinating look at native Florida animals and birds in their natural surroundings.

St. Marks Lighthouse.
The original St. Marks Lighthouse was built in 1829 by Winslow Lewis of Boston for $11,765, but the structure was judged unacceptable because the tower walls were found to be hollow rather than solid. Calvin Knowlton reconstructed the eighty-foot tower using limestone blocks taken from the ruins of old Fort San Marcos de Apalache. The reflector lens, from Paris, was installed in 1829. On a clear evening the light, now triggered by an electric eye, can be seen fifteen miles away.

Wildlife Refuge Highlight—St. Marks Lighthouse

We traveled south on SR 363 and County Road (CR) 59 to the coast. At the end of a scenic drive through St. Marks National Wildlife Refuge (birds and alligators galore) we found St. Marks Lighthouse, one of the oldest (1831) in the southeast. Made of stones from old Fort San Marcos de Apalache, this lighthouse guides ships with the same lens used during the Civil War. (The lens was scratched and chipped when the reflector was hidden in the salt marsh by Confederate troops.) Apparently the lighthouse was well constructed; it survived the terrible storm of September, 1843, when every other building in the area was washed away.

The refuge is only open during daylight hours, so we headed west on US 98 to Panacea, where we found Holiday Camp Ground. This was an ideal overnight stop on three counts: We were tired and hungry, the campground sits on the banks of Ochlockonee Bay, and right across the road is Angelo's Seafood Restaurant. Panacea . . . good name.

Angelo's "Over the Water" Restaurant

We ordered one of Angelo's specials, a drink named "Sex on the Beach" made of vodka, Malibu rum, raspberry schnapps, cranberry, and pineapple juices. That sounded better than the other special—"Erase Your Face." After all, we had a birthday to celebrate and weren't interested in turning our minds to mush.

The restaurant is built out over the water (originally this was done in order to be in a "wet" county), and the spacious wraparound deck proved the perfect place to relax in a rocking chair, sip our cocktails, and watch the sun slip away. The most popular item on the menu according to Arline, Angelo's wife, is the charbroiled grouper, but I couldn't resist the broiled heads-on shrimp fresh off Angelo's boat, accompanied by a salad with special Greek trimming.

Bill, who given the chance would order scallops in the Sahara, pronounced his dinner among the top three in a lifetime. We still cannot figure out who has the patience to shell these tiny delicacies. In this case, good things really did come in small packages. All birthdays should be so scrumptious.

Hugging the gulf on US 98, we drove through Carrabelle, which has the distinction of having the world's smallest police station. Crime must be on permanent vacation in this small community, since the "station" is a phone booth right on the main drag. They tell us a police car often parks beside the booth waiting for the next call. How can you tell the station from a regular phone booth if the car isn't there? This one is adorned with a "Police" sign and an American flag!

Historic Apalachicola

Views of the gulf were tempting us to stop, but we pressed on so we could spend the night on St. Joseph Peninsula near Port St. Joe. En route we made a brief stop in Apalachicola, which is an Indian word for "friendly people on the other side." This town is renowned for its oysters. Oystermen with long-handled tongs take ninety percent of the state's production of oysters from 10,000 well-tended beds.

To export the oysters out of state, oystermen faced a seemingly insurmountable problem: keeping them fresh. Dr. John Gorrie of Apalachicola came up with an answer in 1845 while seeking a way to keep his malaria patients cool. His revolutionary ice-making machine led the way to modern refrigeration and air conditioning. We saw a replica of the first machine, which he finally patented in 1851, on display in the one-room John Gorrie State Museum (at Avenue C and Sixth Street in Apalachicola), as well as exhibits on local history.

Across the street is one of the oldest churches in the state. Trinity Church, one of the first "prefabricated" buildings in Florida, was cut into sections in New York in the 1830s and shipped down the eastern seaboard and around the Florida Keys. The church contributed its original bell, which was melted down to make cannon, to the Confederate cause.

Overnight on St. Joseph Peninsula

St. Joseph Peninsula State Park (also known as T. H. Stone Memorial) is an excellent camping spot. We wanted to be as near the gulf as possible and were fortunate to end up one dune away from the water. Of course, some

Ice was once a precious commodity in Florida. In fact, it had to be shipped all the way from the Great Lakes. Dr. John Gorrie tried valiantly to cool his feverish malaria patients, but the pipes in his experimental air-cooling machine kept clogging with ice. His frustration changed to joy when he realized he had accidentally discovered a way to make ice. This paved the way for modern refrigeration and air conditioning. Dr. Gorrie's original ice-making machine is in the Smithsonian Institution.

Coastal Park.
St. Joseph Peninsula Park is bordered on one side by the Gulf of Mexico and on the other by St. Joseph Bay. The park (also known as T. H. Stone Memorial in honor of one of the original settlers of Port St. Joe), contains small freshwater and salt marshes, freshwater ponds, huge barrier dunes, and one of the most beautiful beaches on the Gulf of Mexico coast.

dunes in this park reach heights of sixty feet so you have to climb a fairly steep boardwalk to get to the beach. But is it worth it! If you like your beaches dazzling white and stretching as far as the eye can see, this is your place. The water was warm, our April weather perfect, and the crowds were somewhere else.

Lively Fishing at Dead Lakes

What is it about RVers? They must have restless blood. Why else would we leave this delightful beach to check out some moribund lakes? Somehow the name "Dead Lakes" did not conjure up visions of the perfect vacation spot. Curiosity won, and we headed north on SR 71. We should know by now not to judge a lake by its name. The Dead Lakes have their own special brand of beauty, and the campground under a canopy of longleaf pines is a haven of tranquility.

The lakes were formed naturally when levees on the Apalachicola River blocked the Chipola River. High water killed trees on the river's

Haunted Forest.
Thousands of dead trees, which give Dead Lakes its unenticing name, create a haunting landscape. This forest of barren cypress, oak, and pine, drowned by the natural overflow of the Chipola River, provides plenty of lively action for anglers.

floodplain, and the trunks of thousands of dead trees give the area its distinctive name and appearance. Most of our fellow RVers were serious anglers who found the lakes anything but dead. In fact, they were literally alive with bass. One fisherman said this was tops on his list of freshwater fishing grounds in the entire panhandle.

We returned to the coast via SR 71 and SR 386 to find the beaches along US 98 getting prettier and prettier. Near Mexico Beach, we could no longer resist the urge to park beside the road and take a dip in the surf. Our decision to overnight in St. Andrews State Recreation Area was influenced by gorgeous views of the gulf as we approached Panama City and rave reviews by RVers we had met on St. Joseph Peninsula.

The Splendors of St. Andrews

They were right. St. Andrews is ideal for sun-and-water worshippers. Brilliant white beaches ease into transparent water that ranges from emerald green to sapphire. This is a popular area for scuba divers because the water is so clear, but you don't need air tanks to enjoy the park. Sandcastle construction crews had some imaginative projects well under way, shell gatherers were filling small buckets, and fishermen on the jetty were becoming selective about what they kept as the day waned.

The best show, however, was at our own back door. Our campsite was in a pine woods directly on Grand Lagoon, where a parade of boats of every description—from elegant yachts to small fishing skiffs—were cruising back and forth. A tall, blue heron walked right in front of us, while out in the bay a mother dolphin was either catching dinner for her baby or teaching it to catch its own fish. The two swam round and round in circles, creating quite a stir in the fish community.

"Did you see the marble sculptures on the jetty?" our campground neighbors asked. That question sent us scurrying back to the beach. It helps to be a mountain goat when you attempt to negotiate the huge boulders that make up the channel seawall. Some of the monster rock chunks used to make the jetty are white marble, and it wasn't hard to imagine a sculptor being lured by the combination of gleaming raw material and grand setting.

We wonder how long it took G. Thompson to carve *Neptune* (dated 1976) and the mermaid (1973), which he had aptly titled *A Place in the Sun.* We like the idea of jetty art, exposed to the elements and appreciated by a few anglers and others who don't mind doing a little scrambling to see it.

A few steps from the fishing pier parking lot is a reconstructed turpentine still. This impressive two-story structure is a remnant of an industry that once flourished in the pine woods of this area. The process by which pine sap was converted into turpentine and resins known as "naval stores" is documented by signs that lead you through the exhibit. Nearby pines show scars from slashes cut in the bark to allow gum to flow into collection containers.

Soaking Up the Sun.
Bounded by the Gulf of Mexico, Ship Channel, and Grand Lagoon, 1,063-acre St. Andrews State Recreation Area, known for its extraordinarily clear water and beautiful white beaches, is one of the most popular outdoor recreation spots in Florida.

St. Andrews with its lily-padded marshes, picturesque dunes, and glorious sunsets was a hard place to leave, but we were assured there were more scenic splendors to the west.

Rolling through Panama City

However, first you have to drive through Panama City's Miracle Strip—a lesson in free enterprise if ever there was one. Fast food offerings encourage a hamburger-, taco-, and pizza-feeding frenzy. How many miniature golf and "kustom" T-shirt airbrushing shops can there be? The answer is an awful lot, plus every other diversion you can think of that will entice the amusement park crowd. When school closes for the summer, this place is jammed. But in April they were just beginning to gear up for the summer. We hummed along thinking the real miracle strip is the glistening white beach across the road. We heard that the nutrient-rich waters teem with blue marlin, sailfish, big bull dolphin, wahoo, and tuna.

The Old South at Eden State Gardens

What a nice contrast to all the hoopla is Eden State Gardens. The mansion and beautifully landscaped grounds are a short hop off US 98 at Point Washington, but it transported us back in time to the days of the Old South. One of the things a prosperous lumber baron did with his money in 1895 was build a great big wooden house with a fireplace in every room. A tour of this lovely plantation home reveals spacious rooms filled with period antiques.

The house, set amid azaleas, moss-draped live oaks, and magnolias, overlooks Choctawhatchee Bay. It's hard to imagine that this serene set-

Stately Mansion.
The Wesley house and Eden State Gardens overlook picturesque Choctawhatchee Bay. According to legend, the house was modeled on a similar Greek-Revival-style dwelling William Henry Wesley stayed in on his way home from the Civil War. Once the hub of a busy sawmill complex, this grand old home, completed in 1898, has a fireplace in each room and a domed cupola with stained-glass windows.

ting was once the heart of a bustling sawmill complex as forests of long-leaf pine and cypress came tumbling down to meet the building demands of a growing region.

Westward on the Emerald Coast Parkway

The Emerald Coast Parkway (toll free despite the fancy name), which had turned inland for a while after Panama City, again treated us to marvelous views of the gulf as we approached Destin. After Destin, US 98, which alternates between two and four lanes along the coast, became once more a four-lane divided highway.

Eglin, at 728 square miles the largest air force base in the world, was much in evidence in the air and on both sides of the road as we neared Pensacola. The base's location was no accident. In 1914, after much study, the government selected Pensacola for its Naval Air Station because it offered so many clear days for flying.

Gulf Islands National Seashore

The weather sounded promising to us so we planned to spend the last few days of our tour at Gulf Islands National Seashore. The Florida section of this seashore includes the Naval Live Oaks Reservation, part of Perdido Key, the forts on the Pensacola Naval Air Station, and part of Santa Rosa Island. This expansive preserve protects, among other things, the barrier islands that shelter Pensacola from storms and hurricanes.

Naval Live Oaks Visitor Center

During a brief stop in the visitor center at Naval Live Oaks we learned how important these majestic trees were to the shipbuilding industry. Besides being resistant to disease and decay, they are the heaviest of all oaks. The *Constitution*, which saw action against the British during the War of 1812, was nicknamed "Old Ironsides" because of the strength of its live oak construction. Because at the time the wood was so highly prized for shipbuilding, the government protected thousands of acres of live oaks in this region.

Signs to Fort Pickens, Santa Rosa Island, and Pensacola Beach led us across the bridge on SR 399. After checking in at the park entrance, we were welcomed by a long reach of windswept dunes sprouting healthy clumps of sea oats. Our campsite was nestled beneath huge live oaks that would have made sturdy ships at one time if they weren't on duty providing us some welcome shade.

By now, we had become accustomed to having gloriously white sands and aquamarine seas almost to ourselves. The gulf shores of northwestern Florida set a new standard for the beachcombing set. But we did have a fleeting concern about becoming hopelessly shriveled if we spent any more time being grilled by the bright April sun.

The live oak has elliptical evergreen leaves, a leathery trunk, and crooked branches. The trees, which grow to forty or fifty feet, are found from southeastern Virginia to Texas. Because they can tolerate salt spray, live oaks are usually found at the edges of salt marshes and in other coastal areas. The wood is extremely heavy, weighing as much as seventy-five pounds per cubic foot.

Mighty Oaks.
Live oaks, once prized for shipbuilding, shade campsites near Fort Pickens in Gulf Island National Seashore at the western end of Santa Rosa Island.

Ruins of Fort Pickens.
Built by the Army Corps of Engineers between 1829 and 1834 to defend Pensacola and the U.S. Navy Shipyard, Fort Pickens was made obsolete by the invention of the rifled cannon, armored battleships, and the advanced technology of late nineteenth-century warfare. The fort is now part of Gulf Islands National Seashore.

By the late nineteenth century, American seacoast forts of brick or stone and earth like Fort Pickens had become obsolete. A new phase of seacoast defenses, reinforced concrete, and earth fortifications continued well into the twentieth century. Both represented a tradition of strong, yet passive, coastal defense. These coastal defenses became obsolete in the early 1940s with an improved navy and air force. Guided missiles and nuclear weapons have replaced the fixed coastal defenses of the past.

Exploring Fort Pickens

We devoted the better part of the next day to exploring the ruins of Fort Pickens on the western tip of Santa Rosa Island. This massive five-sided fort was built in 1834 soon after Florida was ceded to the United States by Spain. Originally designed to protect a Pensacola Bay shipyard, the fort was only attacked once when Confederates tried, unsuccessfully, to capture it during the Civil War.

Perhaps the most unfortunate period in the fort's history were the two years (1886–1888) when Apache chief Geronimo was imprisoned here. He and approximately fifty other Indians had been removed from their former lands in New Mexico and Arizona territories following the last of the United States Apache wars in the Southwest. On weekends people sailed over from Pensacola to taunt the proud Indian who was chained to the fort walls. Exhibits of black-and-white photographs show a stoic chief enduring a sad chapter in our country's history.

The brochure warned of uneven walking surfaces and dimly lit passages and informed us that "small mammals and reptiles inhabit the fort. Please respect animal life and notify a ranger if they inhibit your visit."

Nothing "inhibited our visit" unless we count the mockingbird that accidently flew into the ladies' room and couldn't find the exit. The ranger, when told, was totally unruffled and went for his net. The bird, very much ruffled by five men and women and one small boy in a confined area, all with varying escape-route theories, eventually was netted and released. The ladies' room crowd cheered and waved as the former prisoner winged its way skyward. That's what we like—happy endings!

POINTS OF INTEREST: Florida Tour 2

The Coastal Route

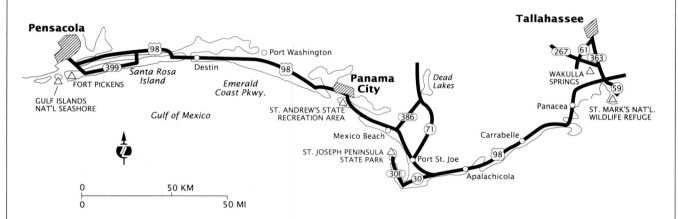

Pensacola · 98 · 399 · Santa Rosa Island · FORT PICKENS · GULF ISLANDS NAT'L SEASHORE · Destin · Emerald Coast Pkwy. · Gulf of Mexico · Port Washington · 98 · ST. ANDREW'S STATE RECREATION AREA · Panama City · Mexico Beach · ST. JOSEPH PENINSULA STATE PARK · Dead Lakes · 386 · 71 · 30E · 30 · Port St. Joe · Apalachicola · 98 · Carrabelle · Panacea · Tallahassee · 267 · 61 · 363 · WAKULLA SPRINGS · 59 · ST. MARK'S NAT'L. WILDLIFE REFUGE

0 — 50 KM
0 — 50 MI

ACCESS: *US 27* to *SR 61* (south of Tallahassee).

INFORMATION: *Tallahassee Chamber of Commerce*, 100 N. Duval Street, Box 1639, Tallahassee, FL 32302 (904) 224-8116; *Apalachicola Chamber of Commerce*, 45 Market Street, Apalachicola, FL 32320 (904) 653-9419; *Panama City Chamber of Commerce*, 12015 West US 98, P.O. Box 9473, Panama City Beach, FL 32407 (904) 234-8224; *Pensacola Visitors Information Center*, 1401 E. Gregory Street, Pensacola, FL 32501 (904) 434-1234.

ANNUAL EVENTS:

Tallahassee: *Spring Farm Days*, Tallahassee Junior Museum (sheep shearing, spring activities, crafts), mid-April; *December on the Farm*, Tallahassee Junior Museum (syrup making, fall activities, crafts), December.

Apalachicola: *Florida Seafood Festival* (oyster shucking contests, blessing of the fleet, etc.), November.

Panama City Beach: *Water Weeks* (power boat race, fishing tournament, sailing regatta), April; *Anderson/Davis International Spring Fishing Tournament*, April; *Deep Sea Fishing Rodeo*, October.

Pensacola: *Mardi Gras* (parades, food festival, musical events, Priscus Ball), five days prior to Ash Wednesday; *Fiesta of the Five Flags* (pageant, parades, art shows, sporting events), May.

MUSEUMS AND GALLERIES:

Tallahassee: *Tallahassee Junior Museum*, 3945 Museum Drive, Tallahassee, FL 32304 (904) 576-1636.

Apalachicola: *John Gorrie Museum* (tribute to the inventor of the ice-making machine), Avenue C and Sixth Street, Apalachicola, FL 32320 (904) 653-9347.

Pensacola: *Fort Pickens Museum and Fort*, Gulf Islands National Seashore, P.O. Box 100, Gulf Breeze, FL 32561 (904) 932-5302.

SPECIAL ATTRACTIONS:

Eden State Gardens, P.O. Box 26 (one mile off US 98 at Point Washington), Point Washington, FL 32454 (904) 231-4214.

OUTFITTERS:

Boat Rentals, *Club Nautico: Destin Yacht Club* (904) 837-6811; *Sandestin Beach Resort* (904) 267-8123; *Ft. Walton Beach* (904) 243-8111.

Skin Diving and Scuba Diving, *Skipper's*, 408 E. Wright Street, Pensacola, FL 32501 (904) 434-0827.

RESTAURANTS:

Angelo's Seafood Restaurant, Panacea at the bridge, Panacea, FL (904) 984-5168.

IN SEARCH OF THE FOUNTAIN OF YOUTH
The Northeastern Coastal Route

*It is a place wonderfull fertill, and of strong
scituation, the ground fat so that it is lekely that it
would bring fourthe wheate and all other corn
twise a yeare . . . yt is a country full of havens,
rivers and islands of suche frutefullnes as cannot
with tonge be expressed . . . the fairest, frute-fullest
and pleasantest of all the worlde . . . .*

Jan Ribaut,
French colonizer, 1563.

For leisurely exploration, it's hard to beat an old, ocean-hugging route like State Road A1A. Shortly after entering the northeast corner of Florida, we left I-95 and headed fifteen miles east for bluer waters—namely, the great Atlantic.

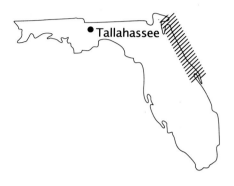

"Marvelously Sweet" Amelia Island

Amelia Island, at the northern border, was the state's first resort destination. The southernmost in a chain of large barrier islands known as the Golden Isles, Amelia's beauty includes both expansive beaches with rolling dunes and lush interior forests. No wonder an English sailor more than 400 years ago described this island as "marvelously sweet, with both marsh and meadow ground, and goodly woods among."

Amelia has had, to say the very least, a turbulent past. This was the only United States location to have been under the rule of eight flags—French, Spanish, English, Patriots, Green Cross of Florida, Mexican, Confederate, and the Stars and Stripes. This is the island the French visited, the Spanish developed, the English named, and the Americans tamed. Today the colorful banners that flutter in the ocean breeze from eight waterfront flagpoles remind the visitor of its varied past.

The island takes a great deal of pride in its extensive list of firsts, including the first driving and bathing beach in Florida, the first city-zoning planning in the United States, the first tourist hotel in Florida, the first (and only) newspaper recording of a Florida bullfight, the first sweet-potato-flour plant in Florida, and the first annual shrimp boat races in the world, to name just a few. Today the major industry is shrimping, which is celebrated at the annual Isle of Eight Flags Shrimp Festival in May. The colorful event features art shows, a mock pirate landing, and the traditional blessing of the shrimp fleet.

Time Warp at Fort Clinch State Park

We camped at Fort Clinch State Park, which commands a splendid view of Georgia's Cumberland Island and the Atlantic Ocean. The park, the most northeasterly point in Florida, takes full advantage of its Atlantic beach, Cumberland Sound, and salt marsh. Besides, it's the only place for RVs on the island. Certainly it boasts one of the most impressive fishing piers (1,500 feet long with night lighting) we have ever seen. If the strings of fish coming off that pier are any indication, Amelia Island is an extremely fertile fishing ground.

The fort is a fascinating reminder of a less-complicated time. Imagine feeling the country was safe as long as its ports were protected. Though this fort was never finished, it saw action during the Civil War and was used for training in the Spanish-American War.

Tour **3** *166 miles*

AMELIA ISLAND • FORT CLINCH STATE PARK • KINGSLEY PLANTATION STATE HISTORIC SITE • FORT CAROLINE NATIONAL MEMORIAL • ST. AUGUSTINE • MATANZAS NATIONAL MONUMENT • TOMOKA STATE PARK • DAYTONA • SUGAR MILL GARDENS • PONCE INLET

Amelia Island was named by British General James Oglethorpe in honor of Princess Amelia, the third child of George II of England.

Bridge of Lions.
The Bridge of Lions, named for the two statues guarding its eastern entrance, crosses Matanzas Bay and connects historic St. Augustine and St. Augustine Beach.

Amelia Seascape.
Amelia Island, the southernmost in a chain of barrier islands known as the Golden Isles, offers thirteen miles of uncrowded beaches complete with towering dunes and a panoramic view of the Atlantic Ocean.

We roamed the ramparts and inspected exhibits in the small museum. Quite by accident, we happened to be there the first weekend of the month when costumed rangers re-enact the 1884 occupation of the fort. These folks really take this time-warp business seriously. They feigned total ignorance when we mentioned computers or men on the moon.

Although busily cooking (a concoction they called "skillygillee") or doing sentry duty, they seemed pleased to take time out to talk to us. We learned, among other things, that the fort was named for General Duncan Lamont Clinch, an important figure in Florida's Seminole War of the 1830s. Occupied by Confederate forces when the Civil War began in 1861, Fort Clinch was retaken by federal troops when a withdrawal was ordered by General Robert E. Lee the following year.

As we were leaving, a soldier stepped in front of us and ordered us to halt. Did we have permission to leave? Well, not exactly. We had to return to the office where a young man laboriously filled out the necessary form with a quill pen. Still not satisfied, the guard at the gate quizzed us as to the president's name. We stammered for a moment, finally came up with "Abraham Lincoln" and only then were granted permission to leave.

Shrimp-Boat-and-Beach Browsing

The next day was one of those that just happen to turn out right. A lot can be said for spontaneity, a pretty place, and good weather. In the morning we poked around the shrimp boats, chatting with amiable deckhands as they mended their nets. Then we browsed in the Fernandina Beach shops, admiring a cheerful clutter of nautical treasures.

Lunch was a platter of boiled shrimp and a cold brew at the Palace Saloon, which claims to be the oldest such establishment in continuous

Fleet's In.
The shrimp fleet drop anchor at Fernandina Beach on Amelia Island. Early in the century, the country's first offshore shrimp trawlers sailed out from these docks. Today, the annual Isle of Eight Flags Shrimp Festival celebrates shrimping as the city's major industry.

operation in Florida (local residents began slaking their thirst here in 1903) as well as "the best bar east of Boise." The afternoon was spent on the beach. You don't often have the run of thirteen miles of uncrowded beach, and we were intent on taking advantage of this rare opportunity. We were happy sunning, reading, and admiring the view until we saw horses in the distance. A beachcomber who had stopped to watch told us this is one of the last places on the east coast where you can still ride horseback on the beach. This was an experience we had to have. Who knew how soon it would be off limits to everyone but beer-commercial makers?

Our stalwart steeds from Seahorse Stable patiently threaded narrow paths through sunken forests of twisted live oaks and palmettos. When they reached the open beach, the horses went straight for the ocean's edge. After an exhilarating ride, we reined to a halt to enjoy the twilight moon. That seascape, complete with fifty-foot dunes and white-crested waves, is indelibly etched in our memories.

Architectural Treasures of Fernandina Beach

The next day we stopped at the chamber of commerce, located in an old waterfront railroad station, and picked up a map of the historic area. The helpful people at the chamber suggested a walking tour as the way to best

Fernandina Beach was once called a "festering fleshpot" by President James Monroe because of the pirates and smugglers who anchored there. It later became Florida's first resort.

Downtown Fernandina.
During the 1870s and 1880s, Fernandina was the terminus on the first cross-state railroad to Cedar Key. Today, the Fernandina Beach Chamber of Commerce is housed in the old depot of the waterfront railroad station.

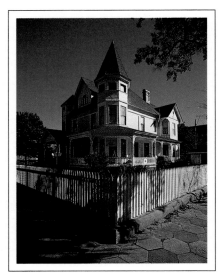

Old Bailey.
The Bailey House (1895) is typical of the Victorian architectural gems located in Centre Street Fernandina, a thirty-block Historic District listed on the National Register of Historic Places. With its turrets, gables, bays, fish-scale decoration, and many windows, the home, which took three years to build and cost a then-outlandish $10,000, is an outstanding example of Queen-Anne style.

appreciate Centre Street Fernandina, a thirty-block Old Town district listed on the National Register of Historic Places.

The first tourist boom, following federal occupation during the Civil War and a massive influx of money from the lumber, phosphate, and shipping industries, created a prosperous seaport in the last quarter of the nineteenth century. Before long, the streets of Fernandina Beach were lined with elegant homes. Toward the end of the nineteenth century, Henry Flagler built his railroad down through Florida, bypassing this island town. Tourism followed the railroad southward, and shipping activity waned. Fortunately, a stagnant economy meant that old buildings weren't leveled, and Fernandina Beach's heritage was preserved.

Strolling gave us the opportunity to appreciate this unusual concentration of late-nineteenth-century Victoriana, ranging from old Steamboat Gothic to Queen-Anne-style architecture. We stopped for a while to watch the meticulous restoration of one gingerbread mansion being reassembled a board at a time.

South on A1A

Leaving Amelia Island and continuing south on A1A, we came to a small sign marking the entrance to Kingsley Plantation. Near the end of a winding road we drove between a row of sabal palms that had been planted by slaves more than 120 years ago.

Although the 1817 plantation house, one of the oldest in Florida and furnished with period antiques, was interesting, we found the long rows of original slave quarters an uncomfortable reminder of a troubling time. Here Zephaniah Kingsley, a Scottish slave trader who made a name for himself by enthusiastically defending the slave system, imported thousands of slaves from Africa and the West Indies, then trained them for specialized tasks to increase their resale value.

Waiting for the Mayport ferry (a ten-minute trip across the St. Johns River that runs every half hour) gave us a sea-gull- and shrimp-boat-watching break and a chance to bone up on what was to come.

The northeast corner of Florida contains a wealth of history. After all, this is where the Spanish explorer Juan Ponce de León first waded ashore and where the oldest continuous settlement was staked out at St. Augustine. As we traveled down A1A we found this country's beginnings were more complicated (and gory) than we had thought.

Ponce de León landed in Florida in April, 1513. He may have been seeking the legendary fountain of youth as the myth says. After all, he was over fifty years old and probably would have welcomed the chance to turn back time. More likely, he was hoping to increase his net worth. Other Spanish explorers had returned from adventurous forays into Central and South America laden with gold. Ponce de León had every reason to think this new land might be similarly endowed: the king of Spain had promised him treasures beyond imagining. All he had to do was find these riches.

Since the expedition landed between St. Augustine and the St. Johns River during the Easter celebration of Pascua Florida (the Feast of Flowers), Ponce de León named the entire region in honor of this holy day. He stayed less than a week, found no magic spring and no yellow metal, but vowed to return.

In 1521 the king commissioned Ponce de León to colonize the "island of Florida" and to attempt to convert the Indians to "our Holy Catholic faith." The Indians found the whole idea entirely unacceptable and eventually attacked the Spanish, mortally wounding Ponce de León.

Spanish bad luck didn't deter the French. In 1562 an expedition led by Jan Ribault first glimpsed the St. Johns River. By 1564 a group of Huguenots (French Protestants) under the leadership of René de Laudonniere erected Fort Caroline on the St. Johns River near the present city of Jacksonville. King Philip was incensed since he considered this to be Spanish territory. He sent Don Pedro Menéndez de Avilés with a sizable armada to rout the intruders.

The Spanish established a base south of the French fort during the Feast of St. Augustine and named their military stronghold as a tribute to that saint. The French, alerted to an impending confrontation, tried a surprise attack by sea but were foiled by a sudden storm. Menéndez marched his troops overland, destroyed the fort, and slaughtered the French, ending their claim to Florida.

The original site of Fort Caroline was washed away after the St. Johns River channel was deepened in 1880. However, Fort Caroline National Memorial, ten miles east of Jacksonville and five miles west of Mayport off SR 10, features a reconstruction of the fort, based on a sixteenth-century sketch by the colony's artist and mapmaker. Commemorating the only French attempt to establish a colony in Florida, this lovely park with its small but fascinating museum provided an enlightening hour's sojourn on our trip south.

The St. Johns River is the only major river in the United States that flows from south to north.

Our Oldest City

St. Augustine is not your ordinary city. The first people we encountered (on the grounds of the public library, no less) were armor-clad combatants flailing away at each other with swords. Dedicated to re-creating medieval battles, they were preparing for a grand contest to be held in another state.

While we had hardly expected to come upon a medieval battle practice, we knew the city was old. Continuously occupied since 1565, St. Augustine was founded forty-two years before the colony at Jamestown was established and fifty-five years before the ocean-weary Pilgrims set foot on Plymouth Rock!

Although sacked by pirates, burned by the British, attacked, counterattacked, and hit with a raging yellow fever epidemic, St. Augustine managed to serve as the capital of colonial East Florida for 280 years. Control shifted from the Spanish to the English, then back to the Spanish,

Ready, Aim, Fire.
A demonstration of old-time firearms is given at Castillo de San Marcos National Monument overlooking Matanzas Bay. Construction of the fort began in 1672, a century before the American Revolution. Symbol of Spain's 235-year presence in Florida, Castillo de San Marcos has never been taken by force, but has changed hands four times by the signing of a treaty.

who finally turned it over to the Americans in 1821. On the advice of a woman in the visitor information center we watched two excellent films that dramatized the settlement's difficult beginnings—*Dream of Empire* and *Struggle to Survive.*

St. Augustine takes great pride in its antiquity. Tourists are urged to visit the oldest store, the oldest school, the oldest wax museum, even the oldest alligator farm. We concentrated on huge Castillo de San Marcos, a national monument overlooking Matanzas Bay where we watched a demonstration of old-time firearms, and St. George Street, an attractive old-world reconstruction of the 1750–1845 period with overhanging balconies and walled gardens. We tromped through restored buildings, sampled an *empanada* (a meat turnover) from the Spanish Bakery, and watched costumed craftsmen dip candles, weave cloth, and roll cigars.

Across the Bridge of Lions

At sundown, we headed across the Bridge of Lions to the beach where we had a reservation at St. Augustine Ocean Resort. Where to eat? The owner steered us down the road to Salt Water Cowboys on the intracoastal waterway. A cigar-smoking raccoon with a cane pole and a gun-totin' possum (fortunately both stuffed) greeted us just inside the door. Indians and early Florida settlers peered out from old black-and-white photographs. Alligator skulls and snake skins adorned the walls, the booths were draped with fishing nets, and the furniture was custom made of willow wood by one "Daddy Sticks."

Surrounded by old Florida memorabilia, we could nibble on alligator tail or down a bucket of steamed oysters. The barbecue promised to be

Serene St. Augustine.
This placid St. Augustine waterfront scene, with the Bridge of Lions in the background, belies a violent history during which the nation's oldest city was attacked, betrayed, pillaged, and burned.

City Hall.
The restored 300-room former Alcazar Hotel, built in 1888 by Florida's railroad mogul, Henry M. Flagler, houses both the Lightner Museum and the municipal offices of the city.

the best "this side of the Suwannee or for that matter, the other side, too." But, feeling more saltwaterish than cowboy, we chose the cucumber fish and shrimp casino—very satisfying choices.

Fort Matanzas National Monument

The next day we continued on A1A, stopping fourteen miles south of St. Augustine at Fort Matanzas National Monument. At the visitor center on Anastasia Island, we learned more about the bloody conflict between France and Spain for control of New World territory. Appropriately, the English translation of Matanzas is "slaughters."

The chink in the armor of St. Augustine's otherwise well-protected location was the Matanzas Inlet. An enemy ship crossing the bar into the Matanzas River could sneak up on the town from the south or sail up the San Sebastian River and attack from the rear. In 1569 the way to defend the settlement's "back door" was to erect a watchtower on Rattlesnake Island where soldiers could take turns scanning the horizon. If a ship were sighted, a runner or a man in a log canoe set out to warn the city.

Later, fear of a British attack led to the construction of a fort on this site. We took advantage of the National Park Service's free ferry for a close-up look. The sturdy stone structure was built by St. Augustine craftsmen, with heavy labor done by convicts and royal slaves. The work went slowly; long piles had to be driven into the mud, and the British and Indians repeatedly tried (unsuccessfully) to stop the construction.

Other Pleasures along A1A

South of St. Augustine, A1A becomes increasingly less congested and more scenic. The beach communities near Jacksonville and St. Augustine were in the midst of a building boom, so it was a relief to see uncluttered ocean views as we drove south.

Just below Marineland (one of Florida's oldest attractions), we stopped to explore Washington Oaks State Gardens and lunch beside the Matanzas River. This land was once part of Belle Vista Plantation, owned by a militia general who commanded troops during the Second Seminole War. A relative of our country's first president (also named George Washington) married the general's daughter, and the general deeded the land to them. The gardens and groves were expanded in 1936 when the chairman of the board of General Electric purchased the property. In 1964 the chairman's widow donated the land and its exotic flowers and plants to the state.

The azaleas and camellias were trying to outdo each other as we wandered beside reflecting pools in the formal gardens. On the ocean side of the park (across the road from the entrance), the state's largest outcropping of coquina rocks creates a picturesque beach scene, but it was the close-up look that grabbed our attention. Low tide revealed tidal pools abrim with a full crew of crabs, starfish, and anemones.

Historic Tomoka State Park

We passed a number of beachfront RV parks as we headed for Tomoka State Park. Tomoka, three miles north of the bridge at Ormond Beach (on the mainland side of the Halifax River), has a rich history as well as an abundance of natural beauty. In 1605, the Spanish governor of Florida sent an expedition to explore the coast south of St. Augustine. The men discovered the Timucuan Indian village of Nocoroco near the confluence of the Tomoka and Halifax rivers. The village chief, Tomokie, has been memorialized by Fred Dana Marsh, "artist, idealist and lover of mankind" (according to the plaque), in an exuberant statue.

We were assigned a site beneath the same ancient live oaks that shel-

RVers' Respite.
At Tomoka State Park, RVers camp beneath the same ancient live oaks that shaded Indian huts nearly 400 years ago. The park, on the site of the Timucuan Indian village of Nocoroco, is near the junction of the Tomoka and Halifax rivers at Ormond Beach.

tered Indian huts nearly 400 years ago. Surrounded by a fish-filled lagoon and protected from hurricanes by a barrier island, this was a fine location for the Native Americans, as well as a handy place for us to stay while seeing the Ormond-Daytona area.

Daytona—Birthplace of Speed

At the turn of the century Daytona was, thanks to Henry Flagler and his Florida East Coast Railway, one of Florida's most popular winter resorts for the well-heeled. Henry Ford, R. E. Olds, Louis Chevrolet, and Alexander Winton could not resist 23 miles of 500-foot-wide, hard-packed sand on the "world's most famous beach." Who really did have the fastest car? In 1903 Winton set a world record of 68 miles per hour. By 1904 the Winter Speed Carnival was drawing entries from across the country. Racers proceeded to set thirteen auto-speed records between 1902 and 1935 (when Sir Malcolm Campbell went 276.82 miles per hour), and the area was appropriately dubbed the "birthplace of speed."

Faster cars and larger crowds gradually outgrew the oval raceway that had been dug into the dunes, and in 1959 Daytona's famous 2½-mile asphalt track was open for business. In addition to hosting well-known races like the Daytona 500 and Firecracker 400, Daytona International Speedway offers daily tours, unless a race or testing is scheduled. We were in Daytona the week before the Daytona 500 and were able to enjoy some of the prerace excitement as well as a few time trials.

We were surprised to find that cars are still allowed on certain sections of Daytona Beach, but the speed limit is a piddling 10 mph. Oh well, our trusty motorhome has never been a serious contender in the swift category.

A Visit to Port Orange

A Tranquil Stroll through Sugar Mill Gardens   The next day, in the mood for something on the quieter side, we drove to Port Orange in search of Sugar Mill Gardens. During the early days of Florida, many sugar and indigo plantations were started in this area, and these remains are one of several such ruins. Surrounded by a serene twelve-acre botanical garden and shaded by huge live oaks, this is a lovely (and free) place for a leisurely stroll. A few discreet dinosaurs, left over from a failed venture known as Bongoland, add a slightly bizarre note to the tranquil setting.

We learned that in 1804 Patrick Dean of the Bahamas established a plantation here on a grant of 995 acres from the Spanish government. Subsequent owners called the plantation Dunlawton (for the Dunn and Lawton families). (The settlement of Port Orange was also first known as Dunlawton.) Sugar was processed here until the mill was partially destroyed in the Second Seminole War of 1836. The mill was rebuilt in the late 1840s, and the vats were used to make salt from seawater for the Confederacy. The extensive system of sugar plantations on Florida's east coast was eventually destroyed by Seminole raids, and the sugar industry in this area never recovered.

After Florida was acquired from Spain by the British in 1763, the area that is now Tomoka State Park became part of the vast land-grant holdings of Richard Oswald, a wealthy English merchant and statesman who helped negotiate the treaty with England after the American Revolution.

Daytona Beach was settled briefly in 1767, but the Seminole War of 1836 made this a hazardous place to live. Settlers did not return to the area until the late 1800s.

During the Second Seminole War (1836) the Mosquito Roarers, a company of Florida militia under Major Benjamin Putnam, engaged a large band of Seminoles pillaging Dunlawton, the sugar plantation on the Halifax River. Heavy fighting ensued but the militiamen were unable to disperse the Indians.

Sugar Mill Gardens.
Sugar Mill Gardens in Port Orange contains plantation ruins of an old English sugar mill surrounded by twelve tranquil acres of botanical gardens.

Stuffed to the Gills at Aunt Catfish's

Some of our best restaurant suggestions have come from fellow RVers. We made a real find, thanks to folks in a motorhome that pulled in beside us at the Sugar Mill Gardens's parking lot. "You're already in Port Orange," the driver said, "and you won't find any better food than at Aunt Catfish's down on the river. Parking's easy. They have two big lots right across the street. Only one warning: You better have a big appetite, or you'll never do justice to the meal."

Apparently, Aunt Catfish's Restaurant is not a well-kept secret; the place was packed. Once seated in comfortable stuffed chairs, we faced a be-wildering array of choices ranging from fresh local shark to catfish finger-lings (which the menu suggested be eaten like corn on the cob).

The salad bar (more aptly described by the restaurant as the cheese, salad, and relish buffet) was a meal in itself that offered—along with all the usuals—grits, baked beans, fresh blueberries, and cornbread. We or-dered a special that included blackened, cajun, lemon pepper, and garlic catfish fillets. The fish was accompanied by a Mexican baked potato skin, a delectable cinnamon roll, and a massive hush puppy. No, of course, we didn't have any room left, but we split a slice of their famous Boatsinker Pie anyway. Wonderful and well named!

Ponce de León Lighthouse

Followers of AIA eventually find themselves dead-ended at one inlet or another. At Ponce Inlet our trip came to a fitting conclusion at Ponce de León Lighthouse. Constructed more than 100 years ago, the commanding

The Ponce de León Lighthouse is the second tallest lighthouse on the East Coast.

Ponce Inlet Beacon.
At 175 feet, Ponce de León Lighthouse (1884) offers a spectacular view of Ponce Inlet, New Smyrna Beach, and the surrounding area. A marine museum displays much of the original lighthouse equipment, and the restored keeper's cottage and several other outlying buildings are open to the public. Today's modern beacon flashes every ten seconds and can be seen for sixteen nautical miles.

Windswept Dunes.
Wild dunes and surging surf at Ponce Inlet Beach tempt travelers to linger long enough to attune themselves to the ancient rhythms of the ocean.

structure remained in service as a faithful guide to Atlantic Ocean mariners until 1970. This historic monument offers small museums in some of the restored keepers' cottages, as well as a panoramic view of the surroundings. The sign at the entrance to Ponce de León Lighthouse reads, "Nothing indicates the Liberality, Prosperity or Intelligence of a Nation more clearly than the Facilities which it Affords for the Safe Approach of the Mariner to its Shores."

Spiffy new boardwalks and picnic shelters wedged between the dunes make the adjacent oceanfront park a real treat. The Atlantic surf surging onto a wild beach never fails to create a powerful seascape.

Whether swimming, strolling the beach, or just gazing out to sea, this is our idea of recreation as it was meant to be—a refreshing revitalization of the spirit.

POINTS OF INTEREST: Florida Tour 3

The Northeastern Coastal Route

ACCESS: *I-95* (north of Jacksonville) to *SR A1A.*

INFORMATION: *Amelia Island—Fernandina Beach Chamber of Commerce,* 102 Centre St., P.O. Box 472, Fernandina Beach, FL 32034 (904) 261-3248; *Jacksonville and Jacksonville Beaches Convention and Visitors Bureau,* 33 S. Hogan St., Jacksonville, FL 32202 (904) 353-9736; *St. Augustine and St. Johns County Chamber of Commerce,* 52 Castillo Drive, P.O. Drawer O, St. Augustine, FL 32085 (904) 829-5681; *Daytona Beach Area Chamber of Commerce,* Box 2775, Daytona Beach, FL 32015 (904) 255-0415.

ANNUAL EVENTS:

Fernandina Beach: *Isle of Eight Flags Shrimp Festival; Union Garrison Weekend* (witness lifestyle of Union soldiers at Fort Clinch State Park), April/May.

St. Augustine: *Blessing of the Shrimp Fleet,* Palm Sunday; *Spanish Night Watch* (candlelight procession down St. George Street commemorating the presence of the Spanish in St. Augustine), mid-June; *Days in Spain* (3-day festival celebrating the founding of St. Augustine), mid-August.

Daytona Beach: *Daytona 500 NAS-CAR Stock Car Race,* February; *Firecracker 400 Stock Car Race,* July 4.

MUSEUMS AND GALLERIES:

Fort George Island: Restored *Kingsley Plantation,* believed to be the oldest plantation house in Florida, is furnished in pre-Civil War style. Guided tours given several times each day. Located on Fort George Island, off A1A (904) 251-3122.

Ponce Inlet: *Ponce de León Inlet Lighthouse and Museum,* S. Peninsula Drive, Ponce Inlet, FL 32019 (904) 761-1821.

SPECIAL ATTRACTIONS:

Fort Caroline National Memorial, 12713 Fort Caroline Road, Jacksonville, FL 32225 (904) 641-7155.

Fort Clinch State Park, 2601 Atlantic Avenue, Fernandina Beach, FL 32034 (904) 261-4212.

Castillo de San Marcos, 1 Castillo Drive, St. Augustine, FL 32084 (on the bayfront) (904) 829-6506.

St. George Street (reconstruction of 18th-century Spanish-colonial village), south of the city gate in St. Augustine.

OUTFITTERS:

Sea Horse Stable, on A1A at the south end of Amelia Island (904) 261-4878.

Sea Love Charters, Camachee Island, St. Augustine, FL 32084 (904) 824-3328. Deep-sea fishing.

Critter Fleet, 4950 S. Peninsula Drive, Ponce Inlet, FL 32019 (904) 767-7676.

Reef Raider/Ocean Reef, Front Street, Ponce Inlet, FL 32019 (904) 767-6000.

Sea Love Marina, 4894 Front Street, Ponce Inlet, FL 32019 (904) 767-3406.

RESTAURANTS:

St. Augustine Beach: *Saltwater Cowboys,* A1A South at Dondaville Road, St. Augustine Beach (904) 471-2332; old Florida charm, seafood, and ribs.

Port Orange: *Aunt Catfish's Restaurant,* 4009 Halifax Drive at the west end of Port Orange Bridge (904) 767-4768; seafood, ribs, generous portions, reasonable prices.

ORANGE GROVES, LAKES, AND HORSES
The Heart of Florida

When I first came to the Creek, and knew the old grove and farmhouse at once as home, there was some terror, such as one feels at the first recognition of a human love, for the joining of persons to place, as of persons to person, is a commitment of shared sorrow, even as to shared joy.

Marjorie Kinnan Rawlings,
on seeing her Cross Creek home for the first time

We started our trip to the heartland of Florida on I-75, but quickly came to our senses and abandoned it in favor of seeing the countryside. The northernmost section of central Florida turned out to be a pleasant mix of pine forests, small towns, and winding rivers. A very different Florida from the popular palm-tree-and-beach version, this one is quieter, with considerably less glitter. The area's beauty is the kind typically associated with the Old South—a rural calm accented by redolent magnolias and moss-draped cypress trees.

Way Down upon the Suwannee River

Of the many rivers wending their ways through the northern part of the state, surely the best known is the Suwannee. Americans all recognize the familiar lyric "way down upon the Swanee River," even if they aren't sure where the river is. The Suwannee, we learned, rises in the Okefenokee Swamp, which straddles the Georgia-Florida border, and meanders its southwesterly way to eventually empty into the Gulf of Mexico.

Stephen Foster was born in Pittsburgh in 1826 and died destitute at the age of 37 in New York City. The songwriter who made the river famous probably had only a hazy notion of its location. He just liked the name and thought it worked well in the song. (Foster sold all the rights to "Old Folks At Home" for $15.) Although he never saw the Suwannee, his memory is honored at the Stephen Foster State Folk Culture Center appropriately located on the river's banks.

We headed for White Springs (three miles east of the interstate at the junction of US 41 and SR 136) and found the Stephen Foster Center to be a refreshing oasis of beauty and song. At regular intervals the carillon tower chimes out a medley of popular Foster songs, including such favorites as "Oh! Suzanna," "Camptown Races," "My Old Kentucky Home," and Florida's state song—"Old Folks at Home."

We strolled lushly landscaped grounds, photographed hoop-skirted women beside the antebellum-style mansion, and inspected Foster memorabilia (including antique musical instruments) in the Foster Museum. We could not possibly turn down an opportunity to experience a little bit of the famous Suwannee so we boarded the *Belle of the Suwannee*, a scaled-down version of the vessels that plied this river in Foster's day, for a twenty-minute cruise.

Adrift on the Ichetucknee

After a pleasant night in O'Leno State Park, we headed south. Below Lake City we again left I-75, this time en route to Ichetucknee Springs State Park (four miles northwest of Fort White off SR 47 and SR 238).

Tour **4** *315 miles*

STEPHEN FOSTER STATE FOLK CULTURE CENTER • ICHETUCKNEE SPRINGS STATE PARK • MARJORIE KINNAN RAWLINGS STATE HISTORIC SITE • OCALA • FLORIDA CITRUS TOWER • CYPRESS GARDENS • BOK TOWER GARDENS • HIGHLANDS HAMMOCK STATE PARK

In the late 1700s the Suwannee River was called the Little San Juan, possibly because a Spanish mission, San Juan de Guacara, was located on its banks. Some historians suspect local dialect changed the name to San Juanee and hence Suwannee. Others believe the river's name was derived from the Creek Indian word Suwani, which means "echo."

Ocala Horse Farm.
The Ocala area, with its majestic live oaks, gently rolling hills, and more than 350 welltended thoroughbred horse farms, has become a mecca for the equestrian set.

"Way Down upon the Suwannee River."
The river made famous by Stephen Foster's famous song "Old Folks at Home" (Florida's state song) rises in the Okefenokee Swamp and meanders through Florida before emptying into the Gulf of Mexico.

As we approached the park, we began to realize something was up. Hundreds of inner tubes lined the roads and seemed to sprout from every gas station. They ranged from tiny to mammoth and formed teetering towers, some as high as twenty feet. Signs promised free delivery and pickup for the price of a rental. Before we had even decided on the half-day or the all-day trip, we were forking over a driver's license and plunking down $2 per tube. (The license was returned when we brought the inner tubes back.) This turned out to be a fine investment. In fact, if anyone ever asks what's the most fun you can have for $2, our vote goes to tubing on the Ichetucknee.

At the entrance we were handed a map showing various tubing options. A park attendant told us the river is often choked with bank-to-bank tubers during the summer. Floating down the Ichetucknee has become so popular the park has had to limit the number of tubers to 1,500 per day to protect the stream's vegetation. If you're not at the park entrance by midmorning on a summer weekend, he said, you might as well forget it.

Food and drink have been banned on the river; no litter marred the pristine stream, and we feel strongly that the resident alligators shouldn't be tempted to alter their dining habits. Also, the park has a lovely picnic area for stoking up on calories prior to launch.

We did our tubing one warm Saturday in early spring and had the river to ourselves. Since the water is a constant 72°F year-round, we were told a chilly day (not unknown in northern Florida) creates the effect of a steambath. We parked all our cares and most of our woes on the banks of this crystalline river, boarded our inner tubes, and dedicated the day to drifting.

The Ichetucknee has to be one of the prettiest streams in the world. We bobbed along beneath an emerald canopy on water as clear as mountain air. Sunlight flickering through streamers of Spanish moss created moving light patterns on the river floor; you could see each fish. One traveled with us for half an hour, others would dart by. We startled a great blue heron that fanned us with massive wings as it passed just over our heads. Early-morning tubers reported seeing beavers and otters at play.

We moved along at a good clip without any effort on our part except for an occasional steering stroke. The current was swift enough to provide a constant change of scene, slow enough to allow us to soak up the serenity. Every turn offered a new view of this dense wilderness studded with cypress knees and limestone outcroppings.

Ichetucknee, which produces 233 million gallons a day, is the state's third largest spring.

A Visit to Cross Creek

Twenty-one miles south of Gainesville on CR 325 (exit I-75 at Micanopy for further directions), we detoured to the tiny community of Cross Creek. We had two reasons to visit the home of Marjorie Kinnan Rawlings: one was her Pulitzer-Prize-winning novel, *The Yearling*; the other was the movie *Cross Creek*.

The novel told a sensitive story of a boy's coming of age in the Ocali, the big scrub country known today as Ocala National Forest. The movie, based on Rawlings's autobiographical book of the same title, tells of a journalist from the north struggling to cope with being suddenly plunked into the untamed semitropical backwoods of central Florida in 1928. She comes to love the setting as well as her "cracker" neighbors and ends up doing her best work here. Even "cracker" food fascinated her, and she compiled a selection of regional recipes in her *Cross Creek Cookery*.

Now a state historic site, Marjorie Kinnan Rawlings's farmhouse is a rambling affair of three different sections loosely held together by porches. Unlike her home in the movie, which took some liberties with the setting, the farmhouse does not overlook a lake.

Mrs. Rawlings's antique typewriter on the front porch seems poised for action. She did most of her writing here, sitting on a deerhide-covered chair behind a large wooden table made from a cabbage-palm log. Her home and its contents have been faithfully preserved, right down to the old-fashioned canned goods on the kitchen shelves, to capture the era in which she worked. In fact, it looks as if Rawlings had just stepped out for a moment.

The property is open daily, except Tuesday and Wednesday, but be aware that the tours given every half hour can accommodate only ten people, and there are no advance reservations for this destination.

Thoroughbred Country

The shaggy cypresses mirrored in the dark creeks of Marjorie Kinnan Rawlings country soon gave way to gently rolling hills, massive oaks, and meticulously manicured horse farms. The Ocala area is not only the fastest growing thoroughbred community in the world but also one of the outstanding places for raising all breeds of horses. Arabians, quarter horses, Morgans, Standardbreds, American saddle horses, Appaloosas, miniature horses, and Clydesdales all respond to the fertile soil, mild climate, and mineral-rich water of central Florida.

Between the elaborate barns and expansive well-tended spreads, we could almost smell the money. And that was before we learned that the total value of the registered horses in the county is estimated to be over a billion dollars and the farms between $1.5 and $2 billion, give or take a few million. During Ocala Week (held annually in early October) over $10 million in thoroughbreds are sold at the large Ocala Breeders Sales Complex. Other sales, held periodically throughout the year, bring in horse breeders from all over the world.

Although a few horse farms still welcome visitors, all require an appointment. A list may be obtained from the Ocala/Marion County Chamber of Commerce on 110 East Silver Springs Road in Ocala, where parking is often a problem. Rather than tying ourselves to a schedule, we had a grand time driving the backroads without either plan or map. The horses we saw seemed to be thoroughly content in spite of their owners' commitment to "fast track" life-styles, and the setting was splendid.

Florida Citrus Tower—An Elevating View

South of Ocala we chose US 27 because it cut right down through the center of the state. Gradually horse farms were replaced by groves of orange trees and a scattering of lakes. We stopped in Clermont to lunch at the Florida Citrus Tower's picnic grounds. The tower used to be surrounded by 17 million citrus trees, but several devastating freezes wreaked havoc on the area; many groves we passed were either dead or consisted mainly of seedlings.

Although the view was not as impressive as it must have been when flourishing groves reached as far as the eye could see, we were glad to have an elevated look at the surrounding land. Florida's flat terrain rarely provides the opportunity to photograph at 425 feet above sea level, so we paid a small fee to take the elevator to the "Crow's Nest," the equivalent, according to the operator, of a twenty-two-story building.

Built of 5 million pounds of concrete and 149,000 pounds of reinforcing steel, the 226-foot Florida Citrus Tower can withstand winds of 190 miles per hour. Opened in 1956, it has had more than 5 million visitors in its first 30 years.

Almost exactly in the center of the state, the tower is sixty miles from both the Atlantic Ocean and the Gulf of Mexico. On a clear day you can see about thirty-five miles, which includes a view of a good sampling of Lake County's 1,442 natural spring-fed lakes.

The tower is a tribute to an industry that has been linked to Florida for a long time. The orange actually originated in southeast Asia and was first introduced to this hemisphere in Haiti by Columbus in 1493. Oranges were brought to St. Augustine, Florida, about 1565 by the first settlers, but citrus growers moved southward after severe freezes in 1835 and 1894. The industry got a boost when Lue Gim Gong, a Chinese immigrant, developed a frost-proof orange that eventually flourished along the Indian River. Visitors know the name well. You don't drive very far in Florida without being assaulted by signs urging you to stop and buy some Indian River fruit.

The carillon tower thoughtfully provided a musical accompaniment for our lunch. Afterward, we poked about the souvenir-laden shops at the base of the tower, where we watched taffy being made and purchased a jar of tangerine marmalade for the galley.

The Citrus Trail

South of the Florida Citrus Tower, US 27 could well be called the citrus trail. Stands along the road offer "bag your own" oranges, grapefruit, and tangerines. Signs urge travelers to stop for free juice and free samples or to see citrus candy being made (Davidson of Dundee). We passed huge truckloads of grapefruit as well as pickups parked by the roadside selling produce off the back deck. There's something reassuring about rolling into Frostproof, Florida, and seeing groves of trees heavy with oranges.

It's also reassuring to see some long stretches of undeveloped land. The scenery ranges from cattle ranches, pine groves, and sky-blue lakes to grasslands where you might expect to see a herd of giraffes loping along. An occasional egret patrolled the median, and we passed more than one great blue heron searching for supper along a water-hyacinth-clogged stream.

Along with citrus goodness, the Sunshine State busily produces all manner of things to buy, including tomatoes, avocados, cantaloupes, pineapples, pecans, and boiled peanuts. One sign announced proudly, "We grow over 40 varieties of Florida fruit." Some of the more resistible deals offered were cypress clocks, pineapple wine, and pineapple toothpaste!

Blooms and Belles

A short detour to SR 540 off US 27 took us to Cypress Gardens near Winter Haven, one of Florida's oldest attractions. Things have changed a lot since our visit many years ago. What we remembered were glorious flowers and water-skiers doing unbelievable stunts. This was long before anyone even dreamed of skiing barefoot.

On a Clear Day.
On a clear day in Clermont, you can see 2,000 square miles of highlands, citrus groves, and lakes from the top of the Florida Citrus Tower.

A View of Cypress Gardens.
Cypress Gardens near Winter Haven provides spectacular vistas that include meticulously groomed grounds, floral displays, and lovely Southern belles.

Now a full-scale theme park, Cypress Gardens has added "Southern Ice" (the only permanent ice show in the southeast), Animal Forest (a fine collection of exotic and endangered animals and birds), Kodak's Island in the Sky (a revolving platform that affords a commanding view of the area), Cypress Junction (billed as the nation's most elaborate model railroad), and a diverse assortment of shops, snack bars, and restaurants.

In addition to boat rides through a maze of landscaped canals, there are synchronized-swimming shows; high-diving and bicycle-stunt-riding demonstrations; and a firework, laser, and lighted fountains show.

Twilight Time.
Lake Eloise, the glittering setting for daredevil water-ski shows during the day and spectacular fireworks displays at night, becomes a tranquil haven at twilight, offering a glimpse of Florida as it once was. Trees shaggy with Spanish moss recall those early days (more than fifty years ago) when Cypress Gardens was a desolate swamp and Dick Pope a young man with a dream of creating a floral wonderland.

The gardens are better than ever. For one thing more than fifty years of growth has produced blazing forty-foot-high backdrops of bougainvillaea. When Dick Pope announced he was going to create a beautiful botanical garden and started draining the cypress swamp in 1936, people thought he was crazy. The press, which originally called him the "Barnum of Botany," "Swami of the Swamp," and the "Maestro of Muck," later dubbed Pope "the Father of Florida Tourism."

Pope, who recently died, saw his beloved gardens blossom beyond even his extravagant vision into a year-round floral display without equal. Ac-

More tropical and subtropical plants grow under natural conditions at Cypress Gardens than at any other botanical garden in the world. More than 8,000 plant varieties from over 75 countries produce over 12 million blooms every year.

cording to horticulturist Norm Freel, "Unlike northern climates, where the normal blooming season is only 6 or 8 weeks, we can provide our visitors with unsurpassed color in a natural setting 365 days a year, without the artificial atmosphere of a conservatory."

The gardens seem to have been designed with a photographer's eye in mind. Everywhere you look striking vistas are highlighted by pretty young girls in hoop skirts carrying parasols. The addition of these Southern belles came about because of a winter freeze that killed the flowers at the entrance. Visitors would drive up, take one look at the dead plants, and, thinking the rest of the park had been similarly stricken, drive on.

Julie Pope, wife of Cypress Gardens's founder Dick Pope, Sr., was in charge while her husband was away serving in the armed forces during World War II. She rounded up several women from the office staff, dressed them in the widest possible skirts to hide the dead flowers, and placed them at the entrance. Enchanted by this welcoming committee of Southern belles, visitors could hardly wait to see the rest of Cypress Gardens.

"But how," we asked one of these young ladies posing in the hot sun, "do you manage to look so fresh and cool?" Don't tell anyone, but the garden bench at Gazebo Hill is air-conditioned!

The "Starlite Spectacular" lived up to its name by featuring a sky full of fireworks and a daring delta-wing flier trailing flares as he sailed through the night from an awesome height. Afterward we bedded down in a nearby Holiday Trav-L-Park, after deciding that with the azaleas at their peak, it would be a shame to miss Bok Tower Gardens.

A Dose of Tranquility

Luckily, Bok Tower was right down the road (on SR 17A off US 27A, north of Lake Wales). We noticed the orange groves growing thicker and more productive as we drove south. The flourishing trees lining the entrance road into Bok Tower Gardens were prime specimens, laden with luscious ripe fruit.

Edward Bok came to the United States from the Netherlands when he was six years old. Although he left school at thirteen, his successful career as an author and editor included the editorship of the *Ladies' Home Journal* from 1889 to 1919. Through all those years he never forgot his grandmother's advice: "Wherever your lives may be cast, make you the world a bit better or more beautiful because you have lived in it." The gardens are Bok's answer to that challenge.

This quiet haven for plants, birds, and people is an oasis of serenity entirely in keeping with the founder's wishes. In 1923 Edward Bok asked landscape architect Frederick Law Olmsted, Jr., to transform Iron Mountain from a sandy hill overgrown with pines and scrub palmettos into a sanctuary of beauty and tranquility.

As the gardens began to take shape, Bok decided to have a carillon tower built like one he remembered from his childhood in the Netherlands. The tower, made of pink and gray marble from Georgia and coquina

After his visit to Bok Tower Gardens, carillonneur Daniel Robins wrote that the sanctuary " . . . provides the most sympathetic setting for a carillon of any instrument which I have played here or in Europe and I think it entirely possible that it is the best setting which remains for an instrument anywhere . . . . What Mr. Bok intended as a sanctuary for wildlife has become, less than forty years later, a sanctuary for the carillon as well."

stone from St. Augustine, houses fifty-three bells ranging in weight from seventeen pounds to nearly twelve tons. In 1929 Bok dedicated this sanctuary and its "Singing Tower," as it is often called, to the American people in a ceremony presided over by President Calvin Coolidge.

Our favorite spot is the Reflection Pool, which mirrors the tower and comes complete with a white swan gliding in and out of the picture, as if on cue. Unlike the showy expanses of brilliant colors at Cypress Gardens, the effect of these shady gardens is more subtle. If you're in the mood for contemplation, this, unquestionably, is the place to come.

Bok Tower Gardens are on the summit of Iron Mountain at an elevation of 295 feet. The mountain is on Florida's ridge, the state's sandy central backbone running from Ocala south to Lake Placid.

Singing Tower.
The Bok Singing Tower and surrounding gardens atop Iron Mountain (near Lake Wales) serve up a welcome dose of serenity.

Scenic Drive.
A four-mile scenic drive winds through the tangled beauty of Highlands Hammock State Park near Sebring. The park preserves an abundance of wildlife in a virgin hardwood forest. Some of the trees have thrived here for over a thousand years.

Fisheating Creek.
The best way to explore cypress-lined Fisheating Creek without disturbing the beautiful birds that live in this wilderness area is by canoe.

Untamed Beauty

Whoever first said "It's a jungle out there" could well have been talking about Highlands Hammock State Park (off US 27, west of Sebring). Here thrives the Florida of old—the lush, swampy salad bar that in prehistoric times quelled the hunger of huge mastodons.

This is the jungle primeval, the primitive precondo Florida that enchants nature lovers and is today in diminishing supply. We could easily envision disillusioned Spanish explorers clanking through the dense undergrowth, steaming under the weight of their armor, as they uncovered only alligators, elegant birds, and exquisite natural beauty where they had hoped to find gold.

We stopped in the interpretive center to inspect a fossilized giant tortoise shell unearthed here in the 1930s. One of the most complete specimens of its kind in existence, this was also one of the last to have lived before the species became extinct seven to ten thousand years ago.

One of Florida's most valuable state parks, Highlands Hammock is a biologically rich mix of hammocks, pine flatwoods, sand pine scrub, cypress swamps, bayheads, and marshes. The great diversity of habitats—resulting from interaction of water level, soil, and climate—has created a fertile area for bird watchers (177 species have been identified in the 3,800-acre park) as well as a marvelous maze of hiking trails.

After a looping drive through the park to get our bearings, we set out to explore. Surely these are some of the best trails in Florida. The United States champion sabal palm appeared fairly regal at ninety feet, and on Big Oak Trail we admired 1,000-year-old oak trees. Wild fruit perfumed the air on Wild Orange Trail. Hickory Trail, Ancient Hammock Trail, and Fern Garden Trail all offer different versions of untamed beauty. But our favorite was the boardwalk meandering through the swamp and along Little Charley Bowlegs Creek, known as Cypress Swamp Trail.

Anhingas, with wings fanned out, decorated the trees along the trail like doves on a Christmas tree except, of course, they were black. Since an anhinga's plumage is not waterproof, it must perch in the sun with wings outstretched to dry its feathers after spearfishing for supper. After watching them swim with bodies submerged and only their snakelike heads and necks protruding, we understood why they are often called snakebirds. We could have easily spent several days in this park, but time was running low so we continued southward on US 27.

Before heading over to Fort Myers to attend a conference, we spent the last night of our trip at Lyke's Fisheating Creek Campground. Sprawled beside a creek and under a huge row of live oaks that could easily have been the entrance to a grand old Southern mansion, the campground is a favorite starting point for both canoe trips and horseback rides.

We signed up for a "professional guided horseback tour through the cypress swamp" (offered only on weekends), which was cancelled because of a downpour. This is the way some trips end—not with a bang, but with a whimper . . . and a good reason to return.

POINTS OF INTEREST: Florida Tour 4

The Heart of Florida

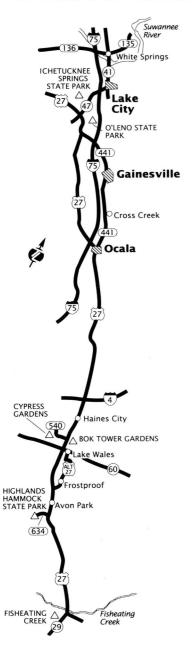

ACCESS: *I-75* (north of Lake City), east on *SR 136*.

INFORMATION: *Ocala/Marion County Chamber of Commerce*, P.O. Box 1210, 110 E. Silver Springs Rd., Ocala, FL 32678 (904) 629-8051; *Winter Haven Chamber of Commerce*, Box 1420, 101 6th St. NW, Winter Haven, FL 33882 (813) 293-2138; *Bok Tower Gardens*, Drawer 3810, Lake Wales, FL 33853 (813) 676-1408.

ANNUAL EVENTS:

White Springs: *Florida Folk Festival* (tale-tellers, musicians, dancers, craftspeople, ethnic foods), late May; *Jeannie Audition & Ball* (auditions for young female vocalists), October.

Winter Haven: *Florida Citrus Festival and Polk County Fair*, mid-February.

Ocala: *Ocala Blueberry Festival*, June.

Sebring: *12 Hours of Sebring Grand Prix of Endurance*, March.

MUSEUMS:

Hawthorne: *Marjorie Kinnan Rawlings State Historic Site*, in Cross Creek off SR 325, Rt. 3, Box 92, 32640 (904) 466-3672.

SPECIAL ATTRACTIONS:

Stephen Foster State Folk Culture Center, at the junction of US 41 and SR 136, White Springs, FL 32096 (904) 397-2733.

Bok Tower Gardens, three miles north of Lake Wales off SR 17A, Drawer 3810, Lake Wales, FL 33853 (813) 676-1408.

Cypress Gardens, three miles southeast of Winter Haven on SR 540, P.O. Box 1, Cypress Gardens, FL 33880 (813) 324-2111.

OUTFITTERS:

Lyke's Fisheating Creek Campground, on US 27 (wildlife and wilderness tours, canoe trips, and horseback guided tours), P.O. Box 100, Palmdale, FL 33944 (813) 675-1852.

RESTAURANTS:

Lake Wales: *Old Europe Restaurant*, Corner 1st Street and Crystal Avenue, Lake Wales, FL 33853 (813) 676-0389.

MICKEY MOUSE AND THE BIG SCRUB
Central Florida

There is nothing on earth comparable to it. We seemed floating through an immense cathedral where white marble columns meet in vast arches overhead and are reflected in the grassy depths below. The dusky plumes of the palmetto . . . looked like fine tracery of a wondrous sculptured roof. . . . Clouds of fragrance were wafted to us from orange groves along the shore; and the transparent depth of the water gave the impression that our boat was moving through the air.

Harriet Beecher Stowe,
on her 1873 visit to Silver Springs, Florida

I f you have overlooked Walt Disney World's Fort Wilderness, you have missed the RVer's promised land. This is certainly not an undiscovered backroad wonder, but if you want to add a lively new dimension to America's most popular attraction, we recommend a stay in Disney's "back lot."

Walt Disney World

Twenty miles southwest of Orlando we exited I-4 (the Walt Disney World exit is clearly marked) onto US 192, drove through the Magic Kingdom Toll Plaza, and followed Fort Wilderness and River Country signs. Our campsite was tucked discreetly into a forest of tall slash pines, cypress, and white-flowering bay trees draped with strands of Spanish moss. Somehow this was not how we pictured Walt Disney World. The question was, Where were all the people? The answer was that they, too, were tucked away into various camping loops in the 740-acre campground.

The beauty of Fort Wilderness is that once you've settled into a campsite, your RV can stay put. Free buses and trams operate every few minutes from a stop a few steps from your campsite, nearby motor launches and buses leave frequently for the Magic Kingdom, and it's easy to transfer to a monorail to reach EPCOT Center.

We were given a packet of information at the gate, and we were starved. The logical thing was to find a place where we could eat and read without having to dress for dinner. Crockett's Tavern, a short bus ride away, was just the ticket. So were the large prawns and the perfectly prepared assortment of fresh vegetables. Davy Crockett's canoe hanging above the tables and his rifle carefully ensconced near the bar added nice touches to the rustic atmosphere.

A bonus to our out-to-eat excursion was that it gave us a chance to get our bearings. The restaurant was in a small complex that included a trading post for groceries and RV supplies, Pioneer Hall (featuring the ever-popular "Hoop-Dee-Doo Revue" dinner show), and the beach area where we learned we could happily spend the day or board a launch for the Magic Kingdom.

You're never finished touring Walt Disney World and EPCOT Center, as we keep finding out. We checked out some of the attractions that had been added since our last visit, including EPCOT Center's Norway Pavilion with its exciting voyage up (!) a white-water rapids into a tenth-century Viking village.

We finally managed to lunch in the Coral Reef Restaurant in Future World's Living Seas (EPCOT Center) where we enjoyed one of the best live shows we've ever seen—a fantastic array of Caribbean reef fish (including a 400-pound tiger shark) cruising a tropical reef a few feet from

Tour **5** *141 miles*

WALT DISNEY WORLD • EPCOT CENTER • MOUNT DORA • OCALA NATIONAL FOREST • ALEXANDER SPRINGS • JUNIPER SPRINGS • SILVER SPRINGS • SALT SPRINGS • ORANGE SPRINGS

EPCOT stands for "Environmental Prototype Community of Tomorrow."

Best of Both Worlds.
EPCOT Center presents Future World and World Showcase in a beautiful and dramatically landscaped setting.

For Sail.
Walt Disney World's Fort Wilderness Campground Resort boasts its very own lake complete with an expansive white-sand beach and regular shuttle boats to the Magic Kingdom.

our table. The food was delicious and the atmosphere impossible to beat (Mickey Mouse in scuba gear waving to us through a school of neon-colored fish from the largest single-tank aquarium in the world), so we were not surprised when the bill fell clearly into the expensive category. Much more than a meal, this was worth every penny.

Of course, we didn't really need to leave Fort Wilderness at all. We found the enormous selection of activities slightly overwhelming. Did we

Fantasy in the Skies.
Fireworks and lasers combine to create
luminous magic over EPCOT Center.

want to water-ski, horseback ride, bike, play tennis, basketball, volleyball, or pitch horsehoes? How about fishing, canoeing, swimming, boating, or just relaxing on the white sand beach? Should we visit the horse barn or join a hayride?

For those suffering from the breakfast blahs, there is always Chip and Dale's Country Morning Jamboree complete with Melvin the Moose and chocolate chip muffins. And every night a dazzling musical light display of sea creatures enlivens Bay Lake.

We were tempted to join a fishing excursion (guide, refreshments, and tackle provided) after hearing a fellow RVer rave about the seven-pound largemouth bass he'd pulled in just that morning. But we ended up opting for Discovery Island and River Country—two unique offerings we were not likely to find elsewhere. River Country is the ideal place for water lovers. With its giant water slides, swirling water flumes, and old-fashioned swimming hole, we found it a completely refreshing antidote for a warm day.

On a slightly less active note, we enjoyed Discovery Island, a zoological park looking for all the world like a South Seas jungle. Curator Charlie Cook told us that all the continents of the world except the polar regions are represented on this lush island. Ambling down a shady path, we were startled by the powerful call of a trumpeter swan (which explains the name) one minute and the shrill laugh of a kookaburra the next. Our favorites were the free-roaming Patagonian cavies (large guinea pigs with rabbitlike faces) and the huge Galapagos tortoises.

Gleaming Gingerbread.
Mount Dora's Donnelly House (1893),
presently serving as a masonic lodge, is
a fine example of Victorian Steamboat
architecture.

A Visit to Mount Dora

After several days in Fort Wilderness, we decided to head north toward
the Ocala National Forest. SR 535 took us to Winter Garden where we
stretched our legs beside an expansive lake and greeted the resident great
blue heron. Turning west on SR 50 we were treated to wide-open vistas,
vast citrus orchards, and rolling sand hills. We entered Lake County,
named for its 1,400 lakes, turned north onto SR 455, drove through
Montverde, and then headed north on SR 561 through Astatula and
Tavares, where we turned right on old US 441 and drove six miles to
Mount Dora.

Don't be fooled by T-shirts that boast, "I climbed Mount Dora." The
town, built on a bluff overlooking Lake Dora, is a scant 184 feet above sea
level. Just thirty miles northwest of Orlando, it seems several worlds away
from the hustle and bustle of that tourist mecca.

We found this a fine place to wander on foot, browsing the many
antique and craft shops and strolling the grounds of Lakeside Inn, a gracious rambling winter resort where President Calvin Coolidge and his
wife stayed in 1930. The inn, built in 1883 and lavishly restored, is listed
on the National Register of Historic Places. They serve a lovely lunch
(including, we were told, a salad that fills the entire head of lettuce in
which it's served).

We found the Mount Dora Chamber of Commerce in the historic old
Seaboard Coast Line Railroad Station at the foot of Alexander Street at
Third Avenue. This attractive, friendly community takes pride in its tiny
Royellou Museum (open sporadically) that is housed in an old jail and
dedicated to local history. The town's prime architectural attraction (at

Fifth Avenue and Donnelly Street) is a three-story, beautifully maintained, heavily gingerbreaded Victorian extravaganza (a wonderful example of Victorian Steamboat architecture) currently serving as a masonic lodge.

We drove north on Donnelly Street to US 441, turned left and found Captain Appleby's restaurant immediately on our left. (Don't turn as soon as you see the restaurant; they've had some dandy accidents on this divided highway. Take the next left beyond the Captain's and head back so you can make a right turn into the entrance. Parking is no problem; some patrons drive 18-wheelers.) Our brief wait was not nearly long enough: Appleby's waiting room is also a mini museum—a fascinating tribute to yesteryear complete with old ice chests, butter churns, antique stoves, and wicker baby buggies.

Feeling fairly ravenous, we downed an appetizer of fried alligator bites dipped in dill sauce and then demolished the tasty Florida Cracker Sampler Platter consisting of chicken, Crab Imperial, fried petite crab, catfish, and a mug of chowder—all washed down with a mason jar of ice tea. As the menu suggests, this particular meal is aimed at "our perspicacious Northern Cousins to let them try all our good easy eatin', at one sittin'!" Mission accomplished.

You cannot get into or out of Captain Appleby's without passing the bakery's big windows. After our feast, I could not believe we were standing there ogling food, but ogle we did as candy, cakes, pies, and giant chocolate chip cookies emerged warm and fragrant from the ovens. Helpless in the face of such terrible temptation, we purchased some cinnamon rolls, the house specialty, for breakfast.

Ocala National Forest

We rolled northward up SR 19 through Eustis, admiring handsome horse farms along the way and stopping to pick up some information at the Ocala National Forest Center. Then, after passing through Umatilla (the entrance to the forest) and Altoona, we turned right on SR 445 to our overnight destination, Alexander Springs.

That large green area on the map labeled Ocala National Forest has intrigued us for years. Covering more than 430,000 acres and known locally as the "Big Scrub," this is the oldest national forest east of the Mississippi River as well as the southernmost in the country. This forest preserve, bounded by the St. Johns and the Oklawaha rivers, contains central highlands, coastal lowlands, swamps, springs, and literally hundreds of lakes and ponds, as well as a great variety of vegetation and wildlife. Our only national forest with subtropical vegetation, Ocala boasts the world's largest stand of sand pine, the only tree capable of growing to usable size in dry sand. The forest is home to one of the state's largest deer herds, as well as such Florida rarities as the southern bald eagle and black bear.

But what attracted us were the forest's famous springs. Florida has more springs than any other state in the country, and they are concentrated in this section of the state. Springs are classified according to volume: A major spring produces 100 cubic feet of water a second or more than 64 million gallons daily. (Of the country's 78 major springs, 27 are in Florida. The combined output of these 27 springs is 76 billion gallons every 24 hours!)

A Stop at Alexander Springs

When we arrived at Alexander Springs, we were relieved to find it living up to its designation as a major spring as it pumps out an impressive 80 million gallons of crystal-clear 72° water daily. After finding a pretty spot for our rig under a canopy of palms and moss-draped pines, we headed for the water.

Frisbees sailed back and forth, picnickers lounged about the large grassy area, and kids were building elaborate sand castles on the beach. Swimmers, snorkelers, and scuba divers churned across the surface of the spring. We donned snorkels and discovered why so many people were

Water, Water Everywhere.
Alexander Springs in Ocala National Forest pumps out eighty million gallons of pellucid water daily, creating a wonderland for swimmers, snorklers, divers, canoeists, and fish.

spending so much time face down. Fish, seemingly oblivious to our presence, swarmed below us in transparent water.

Thoroughly refreshed, we decided to explore the Timucuan Indian Trail. This region was occupied by Indians for at least 10,000 years prior to written records. Remains of prehistoric villages have been found, as well as small artifact-laden areas dedicated to hunting and gathering. Large shell middens along rivers, springs, and creeks tell the tale of thousands of years of shellfish feasts.

The trail, which threaded through the forest of palm, hardwood, and sand pine, was only a little more than a mile, but fascinating interpretive signs slowed us down. We learned, among other things, that the wood from black gum and tupelo gum trees made excellent drums and that Indians killed fish by tossing the poisonous fruit of the buckeye into the creek.

One of the best ways to see the area is by canoe. Our rented craft (available on a first-come, first-served basis) came complete with two glass windows in the bottom so we could view fish life. What a nice touch—our own private glass-bottom-boat tour! As we meandered down this slow-moving stream bordered with blooming water hyacinths, we passed a whole family of raccoons, as well as several alligators dozing in the sun. It was such great fun that we spent half the next day canoeing the seven miles from Alexander Springs to the landing at Forest Route 552.

Juniper Springs and Its Environs

Our Alexander experience definitely whetted our appetites for another spring. We turned left from Alexander Springs onto SR 445, traveled north to SR 40 and headed west to Juniper Springs. "This," the woman at the main gate assured us, "is the prettiest spring in the whole forest."

Juniper Springs is indeed a jewel. Rimmed by a circular stone wall and surrounded by dense semi-tropical forest, this swimming hole is a real stunner. For a while we watched as intrepid teenagers dropped from the limbs of a huge tree into the brilliant cobalt-blue depths. Thunderous splashes as the kids cannonballed into the pool punctuated the rhythmic sounds of an undershot waterwheel almost hidden by foliage.

We learned the old mill was once used to generate power for the campground. An exhibit in the millhouse displays large photos of the spring when it was a tiny pond in a woebegone setting in 1932, the rather dramatic improvement created by the Civilian Conservation Corps in 1935, and dedication ceremonies in 1936. We usually think of civilization as messing up natural beauty, but in this case the place was vastly enhanced.

Two springs in this area, Juniper and nearby Fern Hammock, produce a combined flow of about 20 million gallons of 72° water every day of the year. But statistics don't even hint at their true beauty. Water boils up through clean white sand creating ever-changing formations resembling creamy cumulous clouds. The billowing sand in this watery kaleidoscope never rests.

Down by the Old Mill Stream. Semi-tropical vegetation threatens to engulf the old waterwheel at Juniper Springs in Ocala National Forest. Today the mill, once used to generate power for the campground, serves as an exhibit area.

Crown Jewel of the Big Scrub.
Known for its incredible clarity, pretty
setting, and 72°F water temperature,
Juniper Springs is a favorite with the
swimming-hole set.

Water temperature may remain constant, but the weather changes with
the season. According to the woman at the snack counter, northerners
enthusiastically plunge in year-round, but Floridians wouldn't dream of
swimming during the winter. The local population shows up during the
cooler months, but it is usually to camp, hike, and canoe. (Temperatures
in this national forest during the dry months between November and
February range from 50° to 72°. Summer is warmer, between 70° and 95°,
and wetter.)

Passing close to Juniper Springs, the Ocala Trail (a portion of the Florida Trail) runs the sixty-six-mile length of Ocala National Forest. We were
content to stroll the lush three-quarter-mile nature trail, passing nu-
merous small springs along the way. Our brief encounter with turtles and
birds in this idyllic setting was like just having a single potato chip: we
needed more. Exploring by canoe proved a satisfying answer. Because this
is a one-way trip from Juniper Springs to the bridge on SR 19 (about seven
miles), an early start is recommended. In fact, the concession doesn't rent
canoes past midafternoon.

Juniper Creek begins as a swift, narrow stream almost completely hidden from the sun by dense foliage. After ducking overhanging branches

and negotiating many twists and turns, we were glad to have the stream gradually widen and slow so we could relax and absorb some of the sights. A pair of otters followed us for about a mile, their heads popping up from time to time. After catching glimpses of both alligators and snakes, we understood why rafts, floats, and inner tubes aren't allowed on this pretty stretch of water. We stopped for a picnic along the way, felt eyes on us, and turned to find a deer watching. Cormorants and ibis flew overhead, and herons stalked the shallows.

A Tour of Silver Springs

Much as we usually prefer exploring the wilderness on our own, we found it impossible to bypass the largest limestone artesian spring formation in the world. Silver Springs, one of Florida's oldest attractions, pumps out 800 million gallons of water a day, the greatest long-term measured-average flow of any freshwater group in the state. Besides, it was a short ride twenty miles west of Juniper Springs on SR 40.

Smooth Sailing on Silver Springs. Glass-bottom boats glide over Silver Springs, the largest limestone artesian spring formation in the world. Estimated to be more than 100,000 years old, the main spring produces more than 500,000 gallons of water daily.

Monkeying Around.
Descendants of monkeys used as "extras" in the original Tarzan movies wait patiently for captains of the glass-bottom boats to deliver their "daily bread."

We were in good company; Mary Todd Lincoln, Harriet Beecher Stowe, and William Cullen Bryant, among many others, had made pilgrimages to the famous springs. But they didn't see the wildlife we saw on our jungle cruise—giraffes, ostriches, camels, and a frisky colony of monkeys descended from those used as "extras" in the original Tarzan movies. The squirrels, hands down the most aggressive we've met, were apparently accustomed to handouts from visitors. Attendance had been down the last several days, and they were clearly out of sorts. A super-friendly squirrel is cute until it tries to run up your leg!

No wonder the glass-bottom boat was invented here. Although they must compete with luxuriant gardens and beautifully groomed grounds, the springs are definitely the center of attention. Well they should be. Their amazing clarity gives visitors an extraordinary view into translucent blue depths accented by inquisitive fish and long strands of gracefully waving grass.

A raft of tourist attractions has grown up around the springs, including the International Deer Ranch, an Early American museum with displays of old toys, stagecoaches, and fire engines; and Wild Waters, a theme park with wave pool, flume rides, and miniature golf course. But we were ready to return to the forest and check out Salt Springs.

The Salt Springs Recreation Area

We headed east, retracing SR 40 for a short distance until we reached SR 314. Turning left (north) we drove through at least a million pines and continued north on SR 19 until we reached the Salt Springs Recreation Area entrance. The 200-unit campground, with RVs scattered under huge, moss-draped live oaks, was lovely in the late afternoon shadows. Constructed when the area was privately owned, the facilities include electrical hookups, warm showers, and a dumping station. A restaurant, grocery store, launderette, gas station, and bait-and-tackle shop are located within the Salt Springs area.

Four-mile Salt Springs Run, which empties into Lake George (the state's second-largest lake), is navigable by power boats. (Watch for the occasional slow-moving manatee in these waters.) Although boats and canoes could be rented at the marina, we noticed most folks brought their own. (Campground patrons are welcome to use the two boat ramps.) Fishing enthusiasts reported excellent catches of freshwater as well as saltwater species—largemouth bass, speckled perch (crappy), catfish, bream, striped bass, mullet, blue crab, and giant shrimp.

Lake Kerr General Store and Restaurant, a short drive down SR 314, had the cure for our hunger for something fresh and local. Specialties of the house include 'gator, turtle, frog legs, catfish, steamed crabs, and oysters. Trophy fish and deer horns adorn the walls, the light fixtures are by Busch

Worth Its Salt.
Salt Springs, the largest developed recreation area in Ocala National Forest, attracts RVers who can't decide whether they prefer saltwater or freshwater fishing. Here they can do both!

Turn-of-the-Century Charm.
The historic Orange Springs Country Inn (1908) recalls the early days when Orange Springs was one of the first health resorts in Florida.

beer, the beverage list includes Asti Spumante, and the waitress's T-shirt announces, "I got my crabs at Lake Kerr General Store and Restaurant." How could we miss?

Orange Springs

We left Salt Springs Recreation Area, turning right (north) on SR 19, crossing the Florida Barge Canal and then heading left (west) on State Roads 310 and 315. The tree-lined hamlet of Orange Springs doesn't amount to much, but the Orange Springs Country Inn is a real find.

This historic home (built in 1908) has been lovingly renovated, furnished with high oak beds, and equipped for old-fashioned dining. The wraparound veranda is a fine place to sip a sour, and the dinner menu has a decidedly Florida focus (call [904] 546-2052 to check; they are not always open). The inn, with its Southern hospitality and turn-of-the-century atmosphere, is a pleasant way to take a step back to a more leisurely, gracious era. The addition of hookups on its shady seventeen-acre grounds is a welcome bonus for RVers.

POINTS OF INTEREST: Florida Tour 5

Central Florida

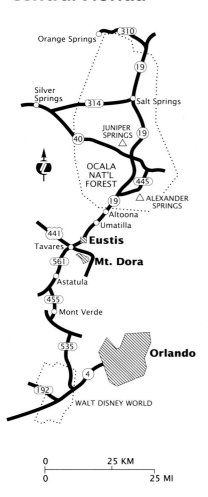

ACCESS: *I-4* (Walt Disney World exit) to *US 192.*

INFORMATION: *Forest Supervisor, USDA-Forest Service,* 227 N. Bronough Street, Suite 4061, Tallahassee, FL 32301 (904) 681-7266; *Lake George District Ranger,* Route 2, Box 701, Silver Springs, FL 32688 (904) 625-2520; *Seminole District Ranger,* 1551 Umatilla Rd., Eustis, FL 32726 (904) 357-3721; *Walt Disney World Central Reservations Office,* P.O. Box 10,100, Lake Buena Vista, FL 32830-0100 (305) 824-8000; *Mount*

Dora Chamber of Commerce, P.O. Box 196, Mount Dora, FL 32757 (904) 383-2165; *Ocala/Marion Chamber of Commerce,* 110 E. Silver Springs Blvd., P.O. Box 1210, Ocala, FL 32678 (904) 629-8051.

ANNUAL EVENTS:

Mount Dora: *Art Festival,* February; *Annual Sailing Regatta, Antique Automobile Show* (pre-WWII autos), April.

Ocala: *Blueberry Festival,* June.

MUSEUMS AND GALLERIES:

Mount Dora: *Royellou Museum,* in former jail and fire station between Fourth and Fifth avenues. Open Wednesday and Saturday; *Mount Dora Center for the Arts,* 138 East Fifth Avenue (904) 383-0880.

SPECIAL ATTRACTIONS:

Silver Springs, a mile east of Ocala on SR 40. Open daily for glass-bottom boat tours and jungle cruises. Also on grounds are *Deer Park, Antique Car Collection, Reptile Institute, Early American Museum* (904) 236-2121.

OUTFITTERS:

Don Combee and R.L. Westbrook, Bass'n Florida Style, Rt. 3, Box 3994, Ft. McCoy, FL 32637 (904) 685-2929.

Oklawaha Outposts, Route 1 Box 1462, Ft. McCoy, FL 32637 (904) 236-4606.

RESTAURANTS:

Orange Springs: *Orange Springs Country Inn,* 1 Main Street, P.O. Box 550, Orange Springs, FL 32682 (904) 546-2052, on SRs 315 and 21 (Florida cuisine in restored country inn).

Salt Springs: *Lake Kerr General Store and Restaurant,* SR 314, Salt Springs, FL 32637 (904) 685-2615 ('gator, turtle, froglegs, catfish, seafood).

Mount Dora: *Capt. Appleby's Inn,* on SR 441 (Florida "cracker" food, seafood, and ribs).

Walt Disney World and EPCOT Center: *Crockett's Tavern, Pioneer Hall, Fort Wilderness, Walt Disney World* (American, rustic atmosphere); *Coral Reef Restaurant, The Living Seas,* EPCOT Center (shellfish, Maine lobster, expensive).

WILD BEACHES, STRANGE CREATURES
The Gulf Coast

*I work when I wants and I sit when I'se feel like it.
Never much worried 'bout where I been, more
'bout where I'se going.*

Silas Dent,
the hermit of Cabbage Key

Our plan was to trundle down Florida's west coast on US 19. Turning off US 19/98, we drove west on SR 320 a short way into Manatee Springs State Park. Since we were thinking Gulf of Mexico on this particular trip, we were slightly surprised to be spending our first night on the Suwannee River.

Manatee Springs State Park

The brochure handed out at the park entrance gate stated that Manatee Springs State Park was an excellent place to canoe, boat, fish, and swim. In fact, it made swimming sound absolutely enticing: "The crystal-clear water of the spring run makes a cool place to swim." After securing a campsite, we donned swimsuits and headed for the spring, eager to test the promise of the advertising.

Then we saw the alligator. To his credit, we must admit the alligator was not actually in the roped-off swimming area. But he was nearby, and he had a sneaky look on his (her?) face. Smack dead center in the middle of the spring run, he was facing the swimming area and heading slowly in that direction. We decided we really weren't all that committed to the idea of plunging into the spring in spite of its refreshing promise. We would have lots of future opportunities to swim and far fewer to alligator watch.

We ambled slowly along the boardwalk leading out to the Suwannee River, keeping our eyes, as well as our telephoto lens, on the 'gator. He wasn't very lively, but he had the confident look of one who's in charge and doesn't need a badge or a title to prove it. No manatees reared their humble heads, but we did see birds, turtles, and lots of high-jumping mullet.

The manatees, according to a park ranger, make rare appearances around the mouth of the run. In 1774 William Barton reported seeing " . . . a continual concorse of fish . . . and the monstrous amphabious maneta, a skeleton of which I saw on the bank of the spring which the Indians had lately killed."

On one side of the boardwalk is the spring run with its considerable current. Manatee Springs produces 116.9 million gallons of water daily. From the springhead, the water flows about 1,200 feet before joining the Suwannee River. Twenty-three miles downstream the Suwannee empties into the Gulf of Mexico.

On the other side, the boardwalk skirts a swamp of cypress, gum, ash, and maple. The combination of twilight and hanging moss gave it an eerie appearance. The spacious campground, shaded by giant live oaks, is a beauty. We could have easily stayed the week, but the open road was calling. We had places to go and manatee to see.

The Sun Also Sets.
The flavor of old Florida lives in the small fishing village of Cedar Key, halfway between Tallahassee and Tampa, but a world apart from both.

Tour 6 *243 miles*

MANATEE SPRINGS STATE PARK • CEDAR KEY • HOMOSASSA SPRINGS • WEEKI WACHEE • TARPON SPRINGS • CALADESI ISLAND STATE PARK • SUNCOAST SEABIRD SANCTUARY • SUNKEN GARDENS • SALVADOR DALI MUSEUM • FORT DE SOTO PARK

The manatee has been hunted for centuries for its meat, bone, hide, and fat. Florida Indians regularly hunted manatees and sold excess meat to the Spanish. Hides were made into leather shields, cords, and shoes, and the ivorylike bones were believed to be of medicinal value. Pioneers arriving in the nineteenth century shot manatees for food. Cowpens Key in the Florida Keys is believed to be so named because manatees were once penned in a small cove there as a food supply.

Off the Deep End.
The boardwalk between the spring run and a swamp of cypress, gum, ash, and maple leads to the Suwannee River at Manatee Springs State Park.

The Flavor of Old Florida

We were following US 19/98 southward when we were seized by an intense desire to see the sun slide into the Gulf of Mexico. Perhaps, we thought, we could indulge our craving for seafood at the same time. We headed west on SR 24 and discovered the perfect place for both sunsets and seafood—Cedar Key.

Surrounded by wilderness, SR 24 provides a look at a Florida visitors never see on postcards. Wildflowers along the roadside add blotches of color to a backdrop of thick clumps of sabal and cabbage palms mingling with pine, cypress, cedar, and mossy oaks. This tangled vegetation, we read, shelters turkeys, deer, wild hogs, and birds of prey. As we approached Cedar Key, the wilderness gave way to waterfront fish markets and a series of bridges. Finally, an expansive horizon announced the Gulf of Mexico.

Cedar Key is far enough off the beaten interstate to have preserved the flavor of Old Florida. Halfway between Tallahassee and Tampa, this tiny fishing village is on the largest of more than 100 islands clustered in the Gulf of Mexico in the curve where Florida's panhandle meets the peninsula. Some nearby keys sport interesting names—Scale, Snake, North Seahorse, and Atsena Otie.

Three miles from the mainland, Cedar Key is officially on Way Key, a 1 by ½-mile island connected to the mainland by causeway. If you can live without a sandy beach, don't need nightlife, and are seeking a reprieve from the frenetic pace of the twentieth century, you will love Cedar Key.

Artists trying to convey the essence of Cedar Key turn out canvases of weathered docks, spindly-legged catwalks, hovering gulls, and fishing boats precariously perched on mud flats at low tide. Is it possible that this was once the second largest city in Florida?

Hard to believe, but trainloads of tourists began to pour into this community in the 1860s after Florida's first major railroad was completed. The railroad, which crossed Florida diagonally from Fernandina in the northeast corner of the state to Cedar Key on the gulf coast, also gave a mighty boost to the local lumber business.

During the Civil War, residents boiled great kettles of seawater to make salt, turning out as many as 150 bushels a day until federal troops abruptly closed down the operation in 1862. After the war, residents turned to shipbuilding and manufacturing wooden pencils. Conservationists were either asleep or overpowered by business interests because the cedar forests, which gave the key its name, were completely sacrificed for the pencil industry. The final "blow" to the area's teetering economy was the destructive hurricane of 1896, from which the area never fully recovered.

With the forests gone, people turned to the sea for their livelihood. The manufacture of brushes and brooms from palmetto fiber looked promising for a while, but the discovery of plastics finished that. Local gift shops sell what is left of the originals. Today the economy depends on commercial fishing and tourism, both on a modest scale.

We learned about this turbulent past at two small museums—Cedar Key State Museum and the Cedar Key Historical Society Museum. The state museum, located on Museum Drive in the northwest part of town, contains both indoor and outdoor exhibits on the area's early history as well as a fine shell collection. Iron kettles used during the Civil War to make salt, old cannons, and iron wagons are displayed about the lawn. The exhibits inside tell the story of the Florida Railroad, the Civil War years, and the lumber industry on Cedar Key. The Historical Society Museum, at Second Street and SR 24, is full of fascinating items contributed by local residents.

In Your Winter Bonnet.
During the winter courting season, the adult brown pelican sports yellow plumage that begins to fade after nesting has begun in the spring. By summertime, the head is pure white, and the bird has a dark brown stripe on the back of the neck.

According to the map, Cedar Key has a national wildlife refuge covering three islands. However, we were disappointed to learn that since the refuge is strictly an environmental-study area, visitors are not allowed. Our disappointment lessened considerably when we learned that we could still see the best of the refuge—the birds—while missing the worst—the rattlesnakes. All we had to do was rent a boat. We had great fun puttering around those small islands glimpsing an occasional roseate spoonbill, and watching pelicans crashing kamikaze-style into the gulf.

Anglers converge on the productive waters of the keys, especially on weekends, and area restaurants take the freshest of the commercial fishing, crabbing, scalloping, and oystering catch. Sufficiently confused by the variety of enthusiastic suggestions from local folks about where to eat, we ended up enjoying a progressive dinner at several restaurants perched over the water.

Along with a panoramic view of the gulf, we indulged in oysters Rockefeller at one lively eatery, a creamy cup of crab bisque at another, and finished off our feast (while totally demolishing our appetites) with turtle steak, stone-crab claws, and a delicate hearts-of-palm salad at yet another restaurant—all within walking distance. We decided there was no need to return to the Cedar Key Seafood Festival in mid-October; we would never be hungry again.

Like the seafood repasts for which Cedar Key is famous, the town is best savored slowly, preferably on foot or by bike. Even with all its nooks and crannies, we found it small enough to get to know in a short time. Besides the memory of a wonderful sunset, we carried away a goodly dose of local charm and seaside tranquility.

Manatee Watching at Homosassa Springs

The chance of seeing manatees is guaranteed at Homosassa Springs Nature World. A friend, who is writing a book on manatees, urged us not to miss this attraction located less than a mile west of US 19. This, she told us, is one of the few places in the world where these gentle giants may be observed at close range.

While the manatees held us spellbound, there are many other reasons to visit Homosassa Springs. Tops on our list were the spring itself, gorgeous birds, and one ungainly hippopotamus named Lucifer.

Lucifer, a movie and television star, has a list of credits that any aspiring actor might envy. He and his sidekick, a pretty white egret, present a startling beauty-and-the-beast contrast to visitors. This massive hippo, who has lived at the spring since he was a year old and is now fifteen, weighs in at 4,000 pounds. His favorite snack? Alfalfa cubes. But of course.

Homosassa Springs Nature World is not a quiet haven. Most of the chatter comes from birds flying freely about, which are used to having people around and don't mind posing for photographs. Flamingos, ducks, swans, geese, snowy egrets, white ibis, great blue herons, and other species from around the world are literally all over the place.

Beauty and the Beast.
Lucifer, a hip hippopotamus who doubles as a television and movie star when not taking it easy at Homosassa Springs, seems to be conversing with his pretty white egret sidekick.

Taking a Breather.
A manatee at Homossassa Springs comes
up for air while munching on the salad
course.

Fine Feathered Friend.
During the nesting season, egrets grow
long feathers called *aigrettes.*

The spring, of course, is the reason for the whole complex. Known as
Giant Fish Bowl Spring or the Spring of 10,000 Fish, it pumps 6 million
gallons of pure water every half hour and serves as the source of the
Homosassa River. The remarkable aspect of this spring is that both saltwater and freshwater fish are found here, a phenomenon scientists are no
better able to explain today than could the Seminole Indians before them.
Depending on the season, as many as thirty-four different species freely
come and go.

The West Indian manatee, or sea cow, is Florida's official marine mammal. Only about 1,000 of these harmless, fascinating creatures now remain, living their peaceful lives in Florida waters. Manatees can live in fresh or saltwater, but apparently need to drink fresh water periodically. They are vegetarians subsisting entirely on aquatic plants. Huge, gentle, and slow-moving, manatees are distantly related to elephants and dugongs. An adult manatee averages between 10 and 12 feet long and may weigh from 1,000 to more than 2,000 pounds.

A unique floating observatory provides a great vantage point to view all this activity. This 168-ton observatory, extending well down into the 55-foot-deep spring, was built—and launched—like a ship. However, fear that the clear spring would be polluted by the grease usually used to slide such a structure into the water prompted the use of bananas as a lubricant instead!

We were able to get a super-close look at an enormous number of fish through plate-glass panels. Sure enough, snook, sheepshead, redfish, jack crevalle, speckled trout, and mangrove snapper mingled with freshwater species such as largemouth bass, bluegill, and bream. At certain times of the year, we were told, giant silver tarpon prowl around the windows observing visitors observing them.

The most thrilling part of being eye level with denizens of the deep was our close-up look at manatees. These strange gray creatures would float by within inches of us like unwieldy floats at a Macy's Thanksgiving Day Parade. We could see each individual hair on their thick, wrinkled hides as clearly as if they were lying on our living room floor.

Better yet, it was mealtime . . . but perhaps it is always mealtime. A vegetarian diet that supports mammals weighing almost a ton must be a never-ending process. Captive manatees have been known to consume as much as 100 pounds a day. No scuba diver ever got a better look at a manatee devouring his salad than we did at our underwater windows.

Each mammal would hold a head of lettuce in its rather small forelimbs and unfurl it one leaf at a time. We had expected them to down great chunks of lettuce, but they nibbled daintily and seemed in no particular hurry. Lettuce was taken in by extending their lip pads out and, with the attached bristles, raking it into the mouth. The food is then chewed by rear molars which are conveniently replaced as they wear down. Later, while watching from shore, we were rewarded with a fine view of a manatee coming up for air with a carrot protruding from its mouth.

The spring, an ideal place for injured and orphaned manatees, has a release program that introduces manatees back into the wild after rehabilitation and boasts the largest captive breeding population in the world. Star, a seventy-pound, forty-three-inch baby girl, the first manatee to be born here, is "ample" indication of the program's success. Homosassa's manatee rehabilitation project operates under the direction of Florida's Department of Natural Resources.

A pontoon boat ride down Pepper Creek introduced us to other residents of Homosassa's Nature World, including a nesting osprey, turkeys, monkeys, and a few goats. Pepper Creek was named for the wild pepper trees on the banks; appropriately the Indian word for "the place of pepper trees" is Homosassa.

Our only disappointment came at Gator Lagoon, where alligators, golden caimans, and a fifteen-foot crocodile are supposed to provide great excitement at feeding time as they "heave themselves out of the water in their frenzy, with huge jaws snapping." One that did saunter over to get a bite to eat obligingly carried a turtle on its back. No frenzy there. Most

Birds of a Feather.
A colony of white ibis forage in the shallows for lunch. Said to taste like chicken, the ibis was once hunted extensively for food by the Indians and early settlers.

seemed about to drown in their own lethargy. The attendant apologized, explaining that it was the wrong time of the year for such goings-on. As the old saying goes, you can lead an alligator to his dinner, but some days you just can't make a high jumper of him.

Between Homosassa Springs and Weeki Wachee, roadside signs on US 19 (a fine divided highway in this section) alerted us to the possibility of bears crossing the road since we were passing through a bear habitat. We kept a watchful eye out to no avail.

Weeki Wachee

Weeki Wachee are Seminole words meaning "little spring," but this 100-foot-wide body of water is actually the surfacing point of a huge underground river. Whatever, it is a real gusher pushing 168 million gallons of water to the surface every twenty-four hours. Divers have yet to locate the bottom of this "spring," which has been explored to a depth of 150 feet and probed another 400 feet with lights.

We boarded a quiet electric-powered boat and took the wilderness cruise through dense tropical foliage down the Weeki Wachee River. Along our winding way we passed an assemblage of personable pelicans at the pelican orphanage, a sort of nursing home (with private pool) for handicapped and permanently crippled birds.

After a brief stop at the exotic bird show where rainbow-colored macaws were literally working for peanuts, we spent a fascinating half hour watching birds of prey display their considerable prowess. These magnificent creatures, which include vultures, hawks, owls, and Mexican caracaras, have been trained but remain untamed. For those able to be completely rehabilitated after injury, this is a way station on the journey back to the wild. In the meantime, it is abundantly clear these are the original masters of aerial acrobatics.

Of course, the prime attraction at Weeki Wachee is the "mermaid" ballet show sixteen feet below the surface of the water where, between acts, a curtain of bubbles shields the "stage" from audience view. We watched in air-conditioned comfort as schools of fish nibbled bread from swimmers' hands, nonchalant turtles cruised by, and a mermaid dove out of sight into the depths of the spring. Working with air hoses, these graceful young women put on a good show, but given a choice, we'd vote for the unwieldy manatees of Homosassa.

The Greek Community of Tarpon Springs

South of New Port Richey, we took US 19A to Tarpon Springs. Good things are happening here, and any sponge diver worth his saltwater will tell you it's about time. The local sponge industry, almost 100 years old, was, until recently, quite decrepit. When Greek immigrant John Cocoris introduced Mediterranean diving techniques here in 1905, sponges thickly carpeted the ocean floor.

After hearing of the rich harvests on Florida's west coast, Greek sponge fishermen packed up their families and traveled to Tarpon Springs. The community prospered as sponging grew to be a multimillion-dollar business and elbowed Key West out as America's Sponge Capital. No one was prepared for the mysterious red tide which practically wiped out the sponge beds in the 1940s. Then customers turned to synthetic sponges, and sponging as a way of life all but disappeared.

We met Angelo Billiris, whose brother George is an international sponge merchant, on the sponge docks after returning from the harbor boat tour and sponge-diving demonstration. He told us the sponge beds

Before Taking the Plunge.
A sponge diver in traditional garb takes a cigarette break prior to donning his heavy metal helmet for the next dive.

are once again flourishing. The number of sponges that they used to harvest in three weeks can now be gathered in half the time. No one is sure why. Angelo speculates that either the disease that killed the sponges is gone, or the sponges have built up an immunity to it.

At the same time, something has happened to the European sponge industry. Experts aren't sure whether the problem can be traced to disease or pollution in the Mediterranean, but suddenly Tarpon Springs sponge merchants have more orders than they can fill. Unlike Americans, Europeans still demand the natural product. Since there are so few divers left, the sponge fishermen of Tarpon Springs are trying to interest sport divers in helping with the harvest.

Sponge gathering is still a tricky business. We were surprised to find that, although wet suits and face masks are preferred for summer sponging, some divers still wear traditional dive suits complete with heavy metal helmet and shoes during the winter. Descending more than 100 feet, never easy, can be downright dangerous. We learned more about the history and vicissitudes of sponging at the Spongeorama Exhibit Center.

While Tarpon Springs suffered the slings and arrows of the sponging industry, it was buoyed up by a steady stream of visitors whose fascination with this colorful Greek community never waned. They stroll the docks along Dodecanese Boulevard (which have been designated a National Historic Landmark), photograph the boats, and patronize spiffy boutiques that have set up shop in the old Sponge Exchange.

Favorite souvenirs are wool or finger sponges, or loofahs for body massages. When their energy flags, strollers simply stop in one of the many Greek coffeehouses and restaurants across from the docks and fortify themselves with some moussaka, Greek salad, and perhaps a glass of retsina wine.

Soaking Up the Sun.
The sponge industry is making a comeback in western Florida. These sponges are for sale near the historic Tarpon Springs Docks.

Greeks Bearing Gifts.
Once used to harvest sponges, this boat is now the centerpiece of a shopping center. The Greek community of Tarpon Springs turned to tourism to boost its economy, which suffered when the sponge beds were decimated by disease in the 1940s.

**Honoring the Patron Saint
of Ships and Seafarers.**
St. Nicholas Greek Orthodox Cathedral
in Tarpon Springs, a fine example of
Neo-Byzantine architecture, is a replica
of St. Sophia's in Constantinople.

No visit to the Greek community is complete without seeing St. Nicholas Greek Orthodox Cathedral on Pinellas Avenue in downtown Tarpon Springs. The community still revolves around the church, which was named for the patron saint of ships and seafarers. A replica of St. Sophia's in Constantinople, this church is an excellent example of New Byzantine architecture with an interior of stained glass, elaborate icons, and sculptured Grecian marble.

Beach Dreaming on Caladesi Island

We decided to stick with US 19A, since we were definitely feeling the need for a beach day. After packing a lunch, we caught the ferry (hourly departures from Dunedin Beach on Honeymoon Island, weather permitting) to Caladesi Island State Park. Accessible only by boat, Caladesi is one of the few remaining undisturbed barrier islands in Florida.

Saved from an extensive condo development in the 1960s, the island consists of a white sandy beach, a mangrove swamp on the bay side (where the ferry lands), and an interior of virgin pine flatwoods and live oak hammocks. While the island has been basically unmolested by humans, nature has taken an active role in its evolution. A 1921 hurricane sliced the island in two, forming Hurricane Pass, which today separates Caladesi from Honeymoon Island to the north.

The word for Caladesi is *pristine*. We walked the two-mile beach but spent most of the day sunning and watching boats go by in the Gulf of Mexico. No wonder sea turtles nest on the beaches during summer nights. This is a fine sanctuary for living creatures, including homo sapiens who need an occasional breather from traffic and time to do nothing more complicated than watch waves.

A Visit to a Wild Bird Hospital

We normally wouldn't interrupt a trip to check on patients at the local hospital, but the Suncoast Seabird Sanctuary in Indian Shores is a unique facility. The parking situation is poor, but it's worth going to the trouble of finding a spot down the road and walking back. This nonprofit organization is known the world over for its dedication to the preservation of wildlife, especially wild birds.

The sanctuary, the largest wild bird hospital in the country, started unofficially on December 3, 1971, when Ralph T. Heath, Jr., found a cormorant walking along Gulf Boulevard dragging a broken wing. Ralph took the bird, whom he named Maynard, to a local veterinarian who after operating returned him to Ralph for recuperation. The word spread, local bait shop owners donated fresh fish, and a steady stream of injured birds began to appear on Ralph's doorstep for care and feeding. Because Maynard's injuries proved to be permanent, Ralph had to obtain a permit to keep a wild bird in captivity.

The sanctuary has come a long way from the days when Maynard hobbled around Ralph's backyard. Today, a full-time staff of wildlife biologists and veterinary technicians provide emergency treatment and care for the birds in a well-equipped hospital complete with intensive care room. Informal tours are offered by staff members.

Approximately ninety percent of all birds brought to the sanctuary have injuries directly or indirectly related to man. Fishing hooks and lines, power lines, pesticides, and environmental pollution have all taken their toll. Treatments have ranged from the fitting of artificial bills on pelicans to the use of orthopedic shoes designed to straighten badly damaged feet.

Hello Polly!
Scarlet macaws say "hi" to visitors at Sunken Gardens in St. Petersburg.

The brown pelican has a very large bill and a prominent, unfeathered throat pouch. Ranging from 24 inches to 54 inches in height, with a wingspread of up to 7½ feet, the bird dives headfirst from heights of 20 to 50 feet to catch fish.

The object is to return the birds to the wild (many thousands have already been released), but those with permanent, crippling injuries are provided a home at the sanctuary or given to highly qualified zoological parks. At times, there are more than 500 land and seabirds at the sanctuary.

Although most of the birds treated are native to the southeast section of the country, none is turned away. The patient list has included such rare migratory species as an Arctic loon, Wilson's stormy petrel, masked booby, white-tailed tropicbird, sooty tern, and a flammulated owl. Some injured birds, who seem to sense that the sanctuary is a safe place, check themselves in by walking right in off the beach.

At Sunken Gardens

More birds were on tap at the Sunken Gardens in St. Petersburg, along with an exotic collection of over 50,000 plants and flowers. Founded in 1903 by plumbing contractor George Turner, Sr., this is the oldest family-owned attraction in Florida and surely one of the most attractive.

It's hard to imagine the good old days when St. Petersburg was a sleepy fishing village on a remote peninsula. Turner arrived in 1902 and purchased some land on a dirt road that featured, as a centerpiece, a large sinkhole and shallow lake. He chose it because his hobby was horticulture, and the property offered a complete cross section of soils, from dry alkaline sand to acid-rich muck.

Turner experimented with a variety of tropical fruits and vegetables, which he sold at a produce stand. As his plant collection grew, so did his desire to use the rich muckland in the middle of his sinkhole. Putting his plumbing expertise to work, George lined the shallow lake with drainage tile and began to reclaim the submerged soil.

Word of his extraordinary collection of plants spread, and churchgoers began routinely detouring through Turner's blossoming backyard after Sunday services. The enterprising horticulturist promptly fenced his yard and charged visitors a nickel to stroll the gardens.

In 1935 George Turner decided to put his other business ventures aside and concentrate on his first love—flowers. He continued to enjoy gardening until his death in 1961. Today his three grandchildren own and operate Sunken Gardens.

Hello Dali

The St. Petersburg area offers so much to see and do that it's sometimes hard to choose. But our next choice was easy. Almost around the corner from Sunken Gardens is the world's largest collection of art by famous Spanish artist Salvador Dali. If you want to take a trip through the mind of a truly complex individual, don't miss the hallucinatory and surrealist images in the Salvador Dali Museum.

Dali's obvious talent as a draftsman, his eccentricity, and his genius are on display in watercolors, drawings, sculptures, objets d'art, and ninety-three major oils. Taking a guided tour or following a printed guide to the

At an 1885 meeting of the American Medical Association in New Orleans, Dr. W. C. Van Bibber presented the results of a ten-year study for the establishment of a "world health city." He concluded that Point Pinellas (the St. Petersburg/Clearwater area) was the ideal location and cited a climate "unequaled anywhere." Few places enjoy as much sun as this area where the sun shines an average of 361 days each year. The Guinness Book of World Records recognizes St. Petersburg as having the longest string of consecutive sunny days: The sun warmed the city for 768 consecutive days, from February 9, 1967, to March 17, 1969.

Drive-in Dali.
Where would an RVer expect to find the world's largest collection of art by famous Spanish artist Salvador Dali? Where else but in St. Petersburg, Florida.

works aids immeasurably in understanding the artist's creative development from 1914 to the present. You'll never again feel the same about grasshoppers or watches.

Since we had overnight reservations at the southern tip of the peninsula, we could take our time. A leisurely dinner en route to Fort De Soto Park was definitely in order, and Silas Dent's on Gulf Boulevard in St. Petersburg Beach turned out to be a fine choice.

The restaurant, named for the hermit of Cabbage Key (now known as Tierra Verde), is a repository of one slice of local history. Silas Dent lived alone on his island in a thatched hut from 1900 to his death in 1952. He would row over to Pass-a-Grille Beach twice a week for supplies and never failed to put in an appearance there at Christmas dressed as Santa Claus. His only worries? Wind, tidal wave, and fire—all of which he experienced and survived. Dent was a man who chose life on his own terms, yet was admired and loved. On his death from leukemia at the age of 76, the *New York Times* carried his obituary.

The popularity of the automobile brought an influx of new travelers to Florida, and in 1921 the forerunner of today's campgrounds was opened in St. Petersburg. Known as Lewis Tent City, it provided guests with bathrooms, laundry facilities, and a grocery store for $12.50 per month for an entire family.

Historic Fort De Soto Park

We reached the end of our trail at Fort De Soto Park. This county park is south of St. Petersburg near the Pinellas Bayway (toll) at the tip of the peninsula. This is an RVer's dream come true—a lush 900-acre setting complete with birds, tropical flowers, a pleasant picnic ground under ancient live oaks, great fishing, three miles of swimming beaches, seven miles of waterfront, fine facilities, and spacious campgrounds. What a splendid base for our exploration of the area.

Cast Your Bait upon the Waters.
Anglers make good use of the day's waning light near Fort DeSoto County Park.

The park sprawls across five islands—Madeline Key, St. Jean Key, St. Christopher Key, Bonne Fortune Key, and the main island, Mullet Key. These were not always the tranquil havens they appear today. Ponce de León anchored off Mullet Key during the summer of 1513 to scrape the barnacles off the bottom of his ship. Attacked by Indians, he was forced to use the ship's cannon in defense of his party. During this fight one of his men, the first white soldier known to be killed in North America, was lost. De León battled once more with the Indians when he returned to Mullet Key in 1521, receiving the wound that eventually caused his death.

Construction of Fort De Soto was completed in 1900 to protect Tampa Bay during the Spanish-American War, but no shot was ever fired at any enemy from the fort. During World War I, it was activated as a Coast Artillery Training Center. Today, it's listed on the National Register of Historic Places, a pleasant spot to view the sunset over the gulf.

POINTS OF INTEREST: Florida Tour 6

The Gulf Coast

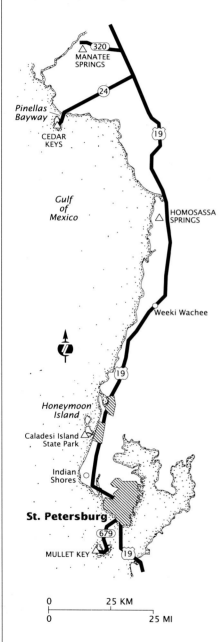

ACCESS: *US 19/98* (west of Gainesville) near the Suwannee River.

INFORMATION: *Chiefland Chamber of Commerce*, P.O. Box 1397, Chiefland, FL 32626 (904) 493-1849; *Cedar Key Area Chamber of Commerce*, Park St. & SR 24, P.O. Box 610, Cedar Key, FL 32625 (904) 543-5600; *Homosassa Springs Area Chamber of Commerce*, P.O. Box 1098, Homosassa Springs, FL 32647 (904) 628-2666; For information on Clearwater Beach, Caledesi Island, Honeymoon Island, Dunedin, Indian Shores, Madeira Beach, St. Petersburg, St. Petersburg Beach, and Tarpon Springs, contact the *Pinellas Suncoast Tourist Development Council*, 2333 East Bay Drive, Suite 109A, Clearwater, FL 33546 (813) 530-6452.

ANNUAL EVENTS:

Cedar Key: *Seafood Festival,* October.

Tarpon Springs: *Epiphany* (Greek Orthodox ceremony, church service, dive for cross, release of white dove, blessing of sponge fleet and day-long celebration with Greek foods and music), January 6; *Greek Wine and Food Festival,* March.

St. Petersburg: *Annual Dinner of the Order of the Salvador* (celebration of Salvador Dali Museum's anniversary), March.

SPECIAL ATTRACTIONS:

Homosassa Springs: *Homosassa Springs,* P.O. Box 189, Homosassa Springs, FL 32647 (904) 628-2311.

Weeki Wachee: *Weeki Wachee Springs,* Box 97, Weeki Wachee, FL 33521 (904) 596-2062.

Indian Shores: *Suncoast Seabird Sanctuary,* 18328 Gulf Boulevard, Indian Shores, Florida 33535 (813) 391-6211.

St. Petersburg: *Sunken Gardens,* 1825 Fourth Street, North, St. Petersburg, FL 33704 (813) 896-3186.

MUSEUMS AND GALLERIES:

St. Petersburg: *The Salvador Dali Museum,* 1000 Third Street S., St. Petersburg, FL 33701 (813) 823-3767.

Cedar Key: *Cedar Key State Museum,* Museum Drive, Cedar Key, FL 32625 (904) 543-5350; *Cedar Key Historical Society Museum,* corner of Second and D streets, Cedar Key, FL 32625.

OUTFITTERS:

Wilson Hubbard, Hubbard's Passport Marina, 150 128th Avenue West, Madeira Beach, FL 33706 (813) 393-1947.

Irwin Hahn, Florida Deep Sea Fishing Incorporated, 801 Pass-A-Grille Way, St. Petersburg Beach, Fl 33705 (813) 360-2082.

RESTAURANTS:

Silas Dent's Restaurant and Oyster Bar, 5501 Gulf Blvd., St. Petersburg Beach, FL 33706 (813) 360-6961.

FROM SARASOTA TO CORKSCREW SWAMP
The Southwest Coast

It is my house. I know what I want and that
is that.

Mable Ringling,
to her architect

F rom our idyllic campsite in Fort De Soto Park, we headed south across the Sunshine Skyway Bridge. This is not your everyday bridge. Modeled after the Brotonne Bridge on the Seine River in France, a little over 4 miles long, it soars 183 feet above Tampa Bay.

Sarasota Bound

Most travelers don't think of Florida as a cultural center. Yet we had recently been privileged to view the world's largest collection of art by Salvador Dali in St. Petersburg. Now we were approaching one of the world's most important collections of baroque art.

Our first stop (off US 41) was Sarasota, and we were immediately impressed by the impact made here by a single man. It's hard to imagine what this community might have been without John Ringling.

Born to a poor German immigrant family, John and his six brothers toured the midwest countryside as musicians. They billed their act as the "Ringling Brothers' Moral, Elevating, Instructive & Fascinating Concert and Variety Performance." Over the years this eventually evolved into the "greatest show on earth," and John became the vastly rich king of the circus.

When he came to Florida in 1909 looking for a winter home, Sarasota was an unsophisticated fishing village with a population of less than a thousand. Ringling, who fell in love with the mild climate and natural beauty of the area, moved his circus winter quarters here in 1927, which, in turn, attracted thousands of visitors. A dramatic transformation took place as John Ringling concentrated his incredible energy, wealth, and creativity on this little village. His aim was to turn Sarasota into nothing less than a great cultural center of the arts.

A Day at the Circus

Although John Ringling is remembered largely as the master of the world's largest circus empire, his most enduring achievement will probably be his contributions to the cultural and artistic worlds. We found ourselves enthusiastic beneficiaries of this rich legacy as we toured the Ringling museums on the sixty-eight-acre estate fronting Sarasota Bay.

In 1927 John Ringling constructed a replica of a fifteenth-century Italian Renaissance palace to house his extraordinary art collection. The rose-colored building flanks a classic 350-foot-long courtyard with columns, fountains, and statuary, including an imposing bronze replica of *David* by Michelangelo. But the museum exterior and surrounding terraces are merely an appetizer.

The John and Mable Ringling Museum of Art, now the State Art Museum of Florida, contains one of the world's most important collections of

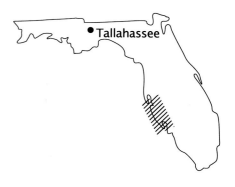

Tour **7** *277 miles*

SARASOTA • RINGLING MUSEUMS • PEACE RIVER • FORT MYERS BEACH • SANIBEL AND CAPTIVA ISLANDS • THOMAS EDISON'S WINTER HOME • CABBAGE KEY • CORKSCREW SWAMP SANCTUARY

Be It Ever So Humble.
There's no place like home, especially if it's John Ringling's residence. The circus tycoon's 30-room Venetian-Gothic mansion (1925–26) was a gift to his wife, Mable.

Frozen in Time.
Renaissance statuary graces the Ringling courtyard sculpture garden.

baroque art, the most complete grouping from Rubens's *Triumph of the Eucharist* series, and an exciting display of contemporary art. When asked why there were so many huge baroque paintings in his collection, Ringling replied, "Because they present man in his boldest, bravest, and most noble aspects." Ringling was far more than a mere collector; he was both a serious student and enlightened connoisseur of art.

In the 1920s Ringling was considered to be one of the ten richest men in the world, with assets totaling roughly $50 million. John and his wife, Mable, put their fortune to work building a colorful Venetian-Gothic palazzo on Sarasota Bay that they called "Ca' d' Zan" ("House of John" in Venetian dialect).

Patterned after the Doges' Palace on the Grand Canal in Venice, their dream home, elaborately furnished with art objects from around the world, cost more than 1.5 million. This sprawling thirty-two-room mansion, with such notable features as a tower inspired by the one on the old Madison Square Garden (an idea that horrified the architect) and a huge crystal chandelier from the lobby of New York's Waldorf Astoria Hotel, is considered one of America's great historic homes.

John Ringling willed his entire estate, including his residence and art museum with all its treasures, to the state of Florida, which now owns and operates the entire complex. In 1948 the state added the Ringling Museum of the Circus to house the richly ornamented circus wagons and huge calliopes from the grand old days of the Big Top. All that are missing are the forty matched horses that used to pull the wagons in Ringling's circus parades.

The state also added an authentic eighteenth-century theater (imported in its entirety from Asolo, Italy) for repertory productions. Opened in 1958, the dazzling theater is often compared to a precious jewel box. One critic wrote in the *Saturday Review* that it was "well worth the price of admission simply to enter and be seated."

Art lovers, circus buffs, antique fanciers, and theatergoers will find it hard to tear themselves away from this remarkable complex. The story of one man's larger-than-life vision captivated us, and we spent the entire day wandering the beautifully landscaped gardens and elegant buildings, with time out for a pleasant lunch break in the screened pavilion on the grounds. This must be one of Florida's best bargains—one ticket provides entry to all four Ringling museums.

Canoeing the Peace River

We detoured off US 41 and headed east on SR 72 toward Arcadia where we had planned a rendezvous with the Peace River. After finding a spot in the Arcadia KOA, we walked next door to check on our reservations at Canoe Outpost. The next morning a young man drove us, our rented canoe, and camping equipment to our launch site upriver at Zolfo Springs.

The Peace was everything the brochures and guidebooks had promised—lush subtropical beauty with plenty of wildlife and a scarcity

The Peaceful Peace.
Adrift on the Peace River, a father provides the rudder while his son waits patiently for a bite.

of people. In four days we saw only a few houses, a revelation for anyone who thinks Florida has completely knuckled under to the condominium craze. We loved the feeling of having the river to ourselves. It's too shallow for powerboats so the only people we saw were a few other canoeists and an occasional fisherman. Expansive cattle ranches lining its banks have prohibited development, making this Florida's most unin-habited natural waterway.

Winding its quiet way from a source in central Florida's Green Swamp to the Gulf of Mexico, the Peace once marked the boundary between Indian territory to the east and white settlers' land to the west. Every bend in the river is a movie set of palmettos, pine, cypress knees, and long strands of gray moss hanging from the gnarled limbs of live oaks.

Wildflowers carpet the banks, and tall water birds stand in the shallows. We saw an armadillo, alligators, herons, egrets, kingfishers, hawks, cor-morants, and ibis, and the sandy banks are imprinted with many deer tracks.

They're in Here Somewhere.
Fossil hunters search the clear waters of
the Peace River.

Colossal Fossil.
This fourteen-pound prehistoric mammoth
tooth was found in the Peace River.

The Peace is a fertile bed for fossil collectors. When we weren't pad-
dling, we were searching the riverbed for fossilized shark teeth. The water
was shallow and perfectly clear, so when we'd come to a good wading
place we'd beach our canoe and begin looking. Our efforts were rewarded with several shark teeth as large as our palms. But the real trophy
was a fourteen-pound tooth that had once belonged to a mammoth, a
prehistoric elephant that inhabited Florida's steaming jungles many thousands of years before.

Canoeists are allowed to overnight anywhere along the bank, so campsites were easy to come by. After dinner we'd incinerate a few marsh-
mallows, then drift off into a dreamless sleep. The Peace River, we
concluded, is very well named.

Gulf Watching at Fort Myers Beach

We returned from Arcadia to US 41 via US 17 and headed for our reserved
campsite in Fort Myers Beach. Red Coconut RV Park, the only such park
in the area right on the Gulf of Mexico, is on Estero Beach. Brochures call
this "the world's safest beach" because of its warm, calm water and gently
sloping sandy bottom. Lots of folks have discovered this lovely seven-mile
stretch of sand, but, even in peak season, the beach never feels crowded.

This is a great place to become a lounge lizard and observe the passing
scene (which beats being a couch potato because we really *were* working—on our tans). Passing dolphins had to compete with soaring frigates,
crash-diving pelicans, ospreys, sandpipers, terns, and ravenous hordes of
gulls for our attention. People in every conceivable attire from Hawaiian

Pelican Hangout.
Boat-watching pelicans perch outside the
Snug Harbor restaurant in Fort Myers
Beach.

muumuus to brief bikinis stroll, jog, bike, sail, windsurf, jet ski, waterski, and parasail by. The beach offers a nice mix of tranquility and action. No wonder many of the RVers we met planned to stay the winter.

As the afternoon waned we decided to brave the traffic and find some seafood. (During the winter Fort Myers Beach has cornered the market on congestion.) The consensus of those here for the duration was to try Snug Harbor, located, oddly enough, at the Fort Myers Beach harbor. Our neighboring RVers cautioned us to hang a left *before* the bridge to the mainland, then take a right and head for the water.

The pelicans hanging around the restaurant obviously knew a good thing when they smelled it. Besides zesty Oysters Casino and delectable scallops, we reveled in the passing parade of sleek boats. Does everyone in the Fort Myers area own a spiffy new yacht? It sure seems that way.

Snug Harbor Restaurant is certainly on the high-tech cutting edge. Our waitress entered orders on a handheld computer which, she explained, were being instantly transferred to the chef. This gave her time to chat with us without holding up progress in the kitchen.

One Day before the Mast.
Pine Island Sound is a vast nautical
playground off Captiva Island.

Sanibel and Captiva—Islands in the Stream

The next morning we rose with the sun, then headed for Sanibel Island. As much as we like Estero Beach, the shelling is better on the other side of the water. After crossing the causeway spanning San Carlos Bay (and forking over a fairly hefty toll), we reached Sanibel Island, internationally famous mecca for shell collectors.

With their beautiful beaches and delightful seaside setting, both Sanibel and Captiva seem ideal island havens for the peace-and-quiet crowd. In fact, it was from Captiva Island that Anne Morrow Lindbergh drew inspiration to write her best-selling book, *A Gift from the Sea.*

Actually, these serene islands have seen their share of violence. Seafaring Indians, rampaging pirates, saltwater floods, and hurricanes all left their marks on these sandy isles. According to legend, pirates once imprisoned a band of women on Isla de las Captivas, which explains why it is now known as Captiva Island.

Hardworking early settlers eked a living from the land and the sea. Their strong tradition of independence and their heirs' preference for isolation died an unwilling death with the construction of the causeway in 1963. This paved the way for the burgeoning resort development still very much in evidence.

A lighthouse completed in 1884 is a reminder of the old days. More interesting than scenic, it guards the eastern tip of Sanibel. A short trail near the parking lot winds through the woods from the gulf to the bay. We found the lighthouse beach fine for swimming and, of course, shelling.

Who can resist picking up a perfectly formed seashell? Certainly we can't. All we had to hear was that Sanibel is one of the three best shelling places on earth. The other two—considerably less accessible to our particular RV—are Jeffreys Bay in Africa and the Sulu Islands in the southwest Pacific.

Sanibel reaches into the gulf rather than hugging the coast in a north-south direction as other nearby barrier islands do, enabling its sloping beaches to snare some of the ocean's most beautiful treasures. Some 400 species end up from time to time on its twenty miles of gulf-washed shoreline.

The best time to shell, we learned, is at low tide during the winter season. We found plenty of coquina, conch, scallop, and clam shells, but ran out of luck when it came to the rarer specimens—the brown speckled junonia, sculpted lion's paw, golden olive, and Scotch bonnet. Of course, our efforts were casual at best, which meant we didn't even begin to bag our limit. (City shelling restrictions prohibit taking more than two live shells per species per person.)

Almost as interesting as their finds are the serious collectors. They tend to walk very slowly, eyes riveted on the sand with bodies bent like question marks in what is known as the "Sanibel Stoop." Collectors love storms, (which stir up their quarry), they tend to be single purposed, and they are not easily distracted. Actually, we found a few of them quite sociable between beachcombings.

Parallel Parking.
Captiva Island offers safe harbor to a
variety of boats.

When the sun was low in the west, we headed for the island's wildlife sanctuary. It's comforting to know that nearly half of the land on these two adjoining islands, Sanibel and Captiva, has been preserved in its natural state. We stopped many times during the five-mile wildlife drive through the J. N. "Ding" Darling National Wildlife Refuge.

Named for an ardent conservationist who also happened to be a Pulitzer-Prize-winning political cartoonist, the refuge protects 4,700 acres of mangrove jungle, tidal flats, lagoons, ponds, and estuaries. A tangle of tropical growth includes cabbage palms, wild orchids, gumbo-limbo, sea-grape, papaya, and strangler fig trees. This mangrove wilderness, strategically located at the southern end of the Atlantic Flyway, is an important way station for migrating birds.

We saw a wealth of wild creatures, including alligators, raccoons, rabbits, and otters. Birds were everywhere, as were marauding squadrons of mosquitoes. In addition to watching the solitary figure of a great blue heron doing a slow strut across a tidal flat and a flock of roseate spoonbills rummaging in the shallows for supper, we were entertained by low-flying pelicans.

An Enlightening Visit

This area is blessed with a fine year-round climate. It's not at all hard to believe that Thomas Edison came to Fort Myers on his doctor's orders. At thirty-eight he was seriously ill, his health suffering from years of overwork. If he wanted to live, his doctor warned him, he would have to escape the brutal northern winters. Edison investigated Fort Myers, liked its warm tropical climate and gulf breezes, and proceeded to lead an enormously productive life to the age of eighty-four. The annual trip was not an easy matter in those days. It involved, among other things, a ten-hour sail from Punta Gorda fifty-two miles to the north. The prescient inventor, who obviously believed the area's attributes far outweighed these inconveniences, declared, "There is only one Fort Myers and 90 million people are going to find it out."

Edison, who spent nearly fifty winters in Fort Myers, is considered the most inventive man who ever lived, holding 1,097 patents for everything from lightbulbs and phonographs to cement and synthetic rubber. Yet there are many facets of Edison's genius we had been unaware of until we toured Edison's home, tropical gardens, museum, and laboratory.

His experiments with rubber are but one small part of the Edison epic. After World War I, the inventor worried about the country's rubber supply. He feared it might be cut off if there were another war. Through crossbreeding he developed a gigantic strain of goldenrod which grew fourteen feet tall and contained as much as twelve percent rubber. In his modest Fort Myers laboratory he pioneered the modern synthetic rubber industry!

We were surprised to find Edison was an accomplished horticulturist. His riverfront garden contains more than a thousand varieties of plants imported from all over the world. Edison wasn't interested in pretty flowers (although he grew plenty of them), but rather in experimenting with the products and byproducts he could derive from unusual plants.

Edison's genius is evident throughout his fourteen-acre Caloosahatchee River estate. Some of the things that fascinated us were Florida's first modern swimming pool (built by Edison in 1900 and still usable), the couch where Edison took his famous catnaps, the inventor's unique Model-T Ford (a gift from his friend Henry Ford), Florida's largest banyan

Edison's winter home and guest house were among the first prefabricated buildings in the United States. Constructed in Maine, they were assembled in Fort Myers after a complicated journey on four schooners.

Biggest Banyan.
Florida's largest banyan tree thrives (along with more than a thousand varieties of plants from around the world) on Thomas Edison's fourteen-acre Caloosahatchee River estate in Fort Myers.

tree, and an electric chandelier with the original carbon-filament light bulbs, which are lit twelve hours every day and still haven't burned out!

Edison contributed much to his beloved Fort Myers. Today, this attractive city is known as the "City of Palms" for the stately rows of royal palms he imported from Cuba and planted on the main boulevard. Shortly after perfecting the electric lamp, Edison offered to provide the entire city with electric street lights. However, the local citizenry was concerned about its cattle. They turned down the generous offer for fear night lights might interfere with their cows' sleep.

The Waters West of Fort Myers

The waters west of Fort Myers are loaded with islands. Sanibel and Captiva are the best known, but we were curious about tiny Cabbage Key. This island, accessible only by boat, is just north of Captiva in Pine Island Sound.

Creative folk seem drawn to the Fort Myers area. Playwright and mystery novelist Mary Roberts Rinehart certainly knew how to keep interruptions to a minimum. In 1938 she built her home atop an ancient Calusa Indian shell mound on Cabbage Key. We booked passage on a lunch cruise, which left from Tween Waters Marina on Captiva Island, and, on arriving at Cabbage Key, felt we had taken a giant step back in time. The writer's home has been kept very much as it was, with a few exceptions.

The house has been converted to an inn with six guest rooms and highly unusual wallpaper; somewhere along the way, people started auto-

Her Island in the Sun.
The island home of mystery novelist Mary Roberts Rinehart (1938), now a six-room inn, was built atop an ancient Calusa Indian shell mound on Cabbage Key.

graphing dollar bills and tacking them on the lounge walls. Current estimates place the value of the wallpaper at around $20,000. The idea is to locate "your" dollar when you return (p.s. Ours is on a rafter).

Corkscrew Swamp Sanctuary

After saying goodbye to our new friends at Red Coconut Park, we headed southward on US 41. Time was running out, but we wanted to catch the wood-stork nesting at Corkscrew Swamp Sanctuary. After leaving US 41, we followed signs to the sanctuary, taking CR 846 east for approximately twenty-one miles. We were glad to have lunch fixings in the galley. The sanctuary has picnic tables, but is basically in the middle of nowhere as far as facilities and services go. Overnight camping, by the way, is not allowed.

After picking up a self-guiding tour book that describes and illustrates the flora and fauna along the way, we took a leisurely 1¾-mile boardwalk stroll through the sanctuary. Helpful staff members at several points along the way answered questions and pointed out some of the more subtle aspects of this fragile environment.

Maintained by the National Audubon Society, this 6,000-acre preserve protects a dwindling population of wood storks. Unfortunately, predictions place the storks close to extinction by the end of this century, with no clear way to save them yet. Though these rare birds are rapidly declining in numbers, due to loss of habitat and human tampering with watershed, this is the country's largest remaining colony of wood storks.

We were fortunate to be there when the birds were nesting and breeding. (This goes on, we were told, from December through March.) Some trees held as many as twenty large nests. The male gathers the sticks for the nests; the female arranges them. If the noise level and frenetic jockeying for space in the trees are any indication, the storks take this business very seriously.

Breeding is timed so food will be plentiful when new storks appear. Only when the water is low will the fish be concentrated enough to provide adequate nourishment for the baby birds. This turns out to be more complicated than it sounds. A single family of wood storks requires 440 pounds of food each breeding season, and water levels in the preserve fluctuate as much as 4½ feet between rainy and dry seasons. A sudden rainstorm at the wrong time brings the whole breeding process to a shattering halt.

We appreciated the shade given by the country's largest stand of virgin bald cypress trees, some more than 600 years old. Bears and bobcats seem to thrive beneath this towering green canopy, though they apparently weren't feeling sociable the day we were there. While wood storks are diminishing in numbers, the Lettuce Lakes had thriving populations of turtles, otters, alligators, and egrets. Thank goodness the conservation movement gathered momentum before the entire state was completely paved over!

POINTS OF INTEREST: Florida Tour 7

The Southwest Coast

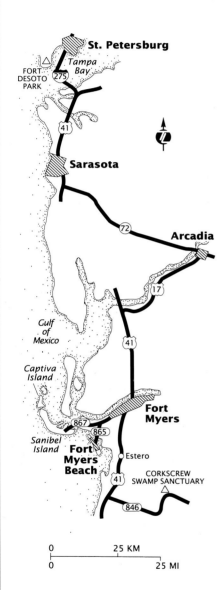

ACCESS: *I-75* (south of St. Petersburg) to *US 41*.

INFORMATION: *Sarasota Tourism Association*, 655 North Tamiami Trail, Sarasota, FL 33577 (813) 957-1877; *De Soto County Chamber of Commerce*, 16 S. Volusia Avenue, P.O. Box 149, Arcadia, FL 33821 (813) 494-4033; *Fort Myers Chamber of Commerce*, P.O. Box CC, 2254 Edwards Drive, Fort Myers, FL 33902 (813) 334-1133; *Fort Myers Beach Chamber of Commerce*, P.O. Box 6109, 1661 Estero Boulevard, Fort Myers Beach, FL 33931 (813) 463-6451; *Lee County Visitors & Convention Bureau*, 2180 W. First Street, Suite 100, P.O. Box 2445, Fort Myers, FL 33902 (800) LEE-ISLE; *Sanibel-Captiva Islands Chamber of Commerce*, P.O. Box 166, Causeway Road, Sanibel Island, FL 33957 (813) 472-3232.

ANNUAL EVENTS:

Sanibel Island: *Sanibel Shell Fair*, March.

Sarasota: *Medieval Fair* (13th-century madrigal singers, jousting, human chess match, crafts and food of the period), March.

Arcadia: *Arcadia Mid-Winter Rodeo* (one of oldest rodeo competitions in the state), March.

Fort Myers: *Edison Pageant of Lights* (ten days of activities—from bike races to doll shows—celebrating Fort Myers's most famous citizen, culminating in Saturday night parade of lights), February.

Fort Myers Beach: *Fort Myers Beach Shrimp Festival*, March.

MUSEUMS AND GALLERIES:

Sarasota: *Ringling Museums*, Box 1838, Sarasota, FL 33578 (813) 355-5101.

Fort Myers: *Edison Winter Home, Garden, and Museum*, 2350 McGregor Blvd., Fort Myers, FL 33901 (813) 334-3614.

SPECIAL ATTRACTIONS:

Naples: *Corkscrew Swamp Sanctuary*, 30 miles northeast of Naples on CR 846, Route 6, Box 1875-A, Naples, FL 33964 (813) 657-3771.

OUTFITTERS:

Peace River Outpost, Rt. 7, Box 301, Arcadia, FL 33821 (813) 494-1215.

RESTAURANTS:

Fort Meyers Beach: *Snug Harbor Seafood Restaurant*, next to the Sky Bridge, 645 San Carlos Blvd., Ft Myers Beach, FL (813) 463-4343 (local favorite for seafood, also steaks and ribs).

Biscayne and the Everglades

*In variety, in brilliance of movement, the fishes
may well compare with the most beautiful
assemblage of birds in tropical climates.*

Louis Agassiz,
nineteenth-century French naturalist,
after a visit to the Florida reefs

The southern tip of Florida offers a two-for-one trip special on national parks. Biscayne National Park and Everglades National Park, a scant twenty-one miles apart, are both summery, water-oriented, wild areas just down the road from Miami. How could we resist?

Biscayne National Park—Saltwater Sanctuary

We headed south toward Homestead on the Florida Turnpike Extension and exited on Tallahassee Road. At the bottom of the exit ramp, we turned left and drove about 3½ miles to an intersection with a stop sign (S.W. 328th Street, also known as North Canal Drive), took another left, and found Biscayne National Park headquarters on Convoy Point at road's end (approximately 4½ miles).

Since most of Biscayne National Park is underwater, the only way to really tour it is by boat. This, by the way, is the largest marine sanctuary administered by the National Park Service. Certainly, the tiny Convoy Point Visitor Center exhibit and few nearby picnic tables are, in themselves, hardly worth the trip. However, a park concessionaire at Convoy Point offers glass-bottom-boat tours and snorkeling trips to the reefs, as well as island excursions for picnicking, camping, and hiking. We selected an "island and bay" cruise and, once launched, were delighted with this pristine area.

Besides a mainland mangrove shoreline, the park protects living coral reefs, a shallow bay, and small tropical islands. No wonder the most popular activities are boating, fishing, snorkeling, and diving. We were amazed by the clarity of the water. Our April day was sunny, but the captain of the boat said that from May through October you could usually count on brief, torrential thunderstorms in the afternoon.

Our first stop was Elliott Key, seven miles across Biscayne Bay from Convoy Point. With its visitor facilities, nature trail, camping, and picnic area, this is obviously the center of activity. We enjoyed the view from the sixty-five-foot lighthouse on the small low-lying island of Boca Chita Cay. We saw splendid birds and learned about strange-sounding trees (gumbo-limbo) and fish (peppermint goby).

All too soon our cruise was over, and we were heading for the Everglades. We could not help envying area residents who had the opportunity to leisurely explore Biscayne Bay in their own boats.

Fruits and Veggies to Go

We found a sprawling fruit-and-vegetable stand southwest of Homestead and Florida City on our way to Everglades National Park and decided to restock the galley. The name of the stand is "Robert Is Here," and, sure

Tour 8   204 miles

BISCAYNE NATIONAL PARK • EVERGLADES NATIONAL PARK • TAMIAMI TRAIL • MICCOSUKEE INDIAN VILLAGE • TEN THOUSAND ISLANDS AREA OF EVERGLADES NATIONAL PARK

In 1960 two developments were planned for the area that Biscayne National Park now protects. Opposition to these development proposals led to the establishment of Biscayne National Monument in 1968. In 1980 Congress enlarged the boundaries and declared Biscayne the forty-seventh national park in the United States.

Gliding Through the Glades.
Canoeists paddle the saltwater byways of a mangrove forest in Everglades National Park.

Boca Chita Beacon.
This attractive sixty-five-foot lighthouse on
Boca Chita Cay in Biscayne National Park
is intermittently open to the public.

enough, he was. When Robert was a kid, his father let him open a roadside stand to sell some of the excess produce from their farm. The business mushroomed, and Robert, many years later, is still going strong. He
obviously likes what he's doing since he couldn't wait to show us his
papaya patch, tell us how to eat a mango, and cut open a starfruit so we
could see the star-shaped cross-section. We loaded up the refrigerator and
bought ice cream cones carefully selected from a long list of tropical
flavors.

As we left, Robert had some sage advice. "A lot of folks are disappointed in the Everglades," he explained. "They don't know what to expect. This isn't dramatic like Yellowstone or the Grand Canyon. They don't spend enough time to appreciate what's here, and they often miss the best part of all, the Royal Palm area. Those who get out of their cars and explore come back again and again. This place is really fantastic!"

The highest point in Everglades National Park is ten feet above sea level.

To Flamingo through the Everglades

Promising not to bypass the Royal Palm area, we proceeded down the thirty-eight-mile road (SR 9336) that ends in Flamingo, where we planned to stay a few days. The main visitor center offers a film explaining the interrelationships between man and nature in the Everglades, as well as pertinent leaflets, maps, and books. We pulled over at all the designated stops along the road, taking in every sight from the wading birds along the Anhinga Trail to the world's largest concentration of saw grass at the Pa-hay-okee Overlook. Pa-hay-okee, which means "grassy waters," was the Indians' name for the Everglades.

Everglades National Park encompasses 1.4 million acres, making it larger than the state of Delaware.

The park campground in Flamingo offers restrooms, cold-water showers, picnic tables, and grills but no electrical, water, or sewage hookups. No problem. After a night in the campground, we planned to leave our rig and delve even deeper into the Glades.

Houseboating the Wilderness Waterway

After our too-brief look at Biscayne National Park, we were determined not to do the Everglades as quickly. Influenced by friends who had been highly enthusiastic about their Everglades experience, we decided to rent a houseboat for the weekend. "You have to be out in the midst of it for sunrise as well as sunset, to spend quiet time and let the Everglades open themselves to you," they had urged.

Good advice. We found the Everglades abrim with the unexpected. Neither of us could say exactly how we thought the area would look, but both of us agreed it was far different from anything we had imagined. For one thing, we had no idea what a mangrove forest would look like. I guess we were thinking of a more junglelike setting like the old Tarzan movies. Also, we were surprised to be cruising in saltwater, complete with tides.

We wanted a wilderness cruise—after all, this is the country's largest remaining subtropical wilderness—and were delighted to see so few boats. But to find the ninety-nine-mile Wilderness Waterway so well marked exceeded our expectations. And we hadn't thought the water would be so shallow. Our boat drew 3 feet and we were running most of the time in 3½ to 5 feet of water. We came to regard 7 to 10 feet of water as really deep. "If the boat sinks," Bill said cheerily, "we'll just go sit on the roof."

We were sure there was a reason for the rivers to have names like Shark and Little Shark. And we had counted on seeing alligators, so we knew we wouldn't be swimming. In fact, we thought we would roast. But it was

Room with a View.
An owl peers from his high-rise deep in the Everglades. The national park, which came into being when the Audubon Society resolved to stop the plume hunters' slaughter of egrets, is a sanctuary for more than 300 species of birds.

Wilderness Waterway.
Houseboating is an ideal way to explore
the rivers and bays that make up so much
of the mysterious Everglades.

*Everglades National Park naturalists give
hikes, talks, canoe trips, tram tours, demonstrations, and campfire programs
during the year. Activities change daily.
One day there may be a sunrise bird
walk, a paddle out into Florida Bay, a
crosscountry slough slog, or a moonlight
tram tour. Ask at the visitor centers for
schedules.*

very comfortable summer weather, always breezy, and we slept under a
blanket, which was certainly contrary to our idea of April in southernmost Florida.

The beauty of houseboating, much like RVing, is that it permits us to
be totally scheduleless. With meals and beds handy, there isn't any pres-
sure to get anywhere at any special time. We were making buoy-to-buoy
decisions about which way to go when a pair of dolphins appeared and
led us out to Ponce de León Bay. Thanks to those dolphins, we spent a

lovely afternoon there, lunching on the top deck and savoring a magnificent view of the Gulf of Mexico.

A restful feature of houseboating in the Glades for us is that we never had to dock the boat or maneuver in and out of a slip. All we did was lower the anchor at night and avoid tree stumps by day. Evening was a special time when flocks of birds were silhouetted in the sinking sun. Incredibly awkward pelicans, who never did get the knack of tree landings, provided comic relief.

One night when the wind came up, we went outside to check the anchor line. Not only was everything okay, but Whitewater Bay had been tranformed into a "wondersea." A storm was churning up phosphorescence everywhere, and every wave was luminescent. Each raindrop hit with a sparkle, until it looked as though the whole Milky Way was spread out before us.

As we cruised the Wilderness Waterway, we passed through salt-, brackish-, and freshwater zones. Gradually, we began to understand what water means to the Everglades. It is the one indispensable ingredient to its ecosystem—the key to its life.

The River of Grass

For thousands of years summer rains flooded the Glades flowing south and west toward the Gulf of Mexico in a "river of grass." Fifty miles wide and a scant six inches deep, this is the widest river in the world. Here fresh water mixes with saltwater to create a nutrient-rich biologic soup, the foundation of the food chain that supports much of the fish in the Gulf of Mexico and along the Eastern Seaboard.

Portrait of an Ace Fisherman.
From heights up to sixty feet, brown pelicans make headlong dives into the sea after their only food—fish.

River of Grass.
The Indians named this area Pa-hay-okee, or "grassy waters." Everglades National Park preserves the world's largest concentration of saw grass as well as the world's widest river, the fifty-mile-wide, six-inch-deep "river of grass."

Saw grass is one of the oldest sedges known. Unlike regular grass, which has a hollow stem, sedge has a solid triangular stem. Blades of this plant are edged with razor-sharp, sawlike teeth.

In the past the wildlife in the Glades survived the dry season because the waters in the north around Lake Okeechobee still flowed slowly southward through the saw grass—the "river of grass"—for three to four months after the rains had stopped. Today, canals and levees around the lake and in the flood-control areas north and east of the park divert normal excess waters to the Atlantic Ocean and the Gulf of Mexico. This shortens the time the water covers the Glades, reducing production of aquatic organisms and in turn bird, fish, and animal populations.

Whitewater Bay has a higher salinity today than it did fifty years ago when saw grass extended to its northern edge. Where once the fresh-water mass held back the saltwater from the Gulf, now saline or brackish waters extend farther and farther inland, and the saltwater-tolerant mangrove trees have taken over.

When President Truman dedicated the park in 1947 he said, "We have permanently safeguarded an irreplaceable primitive area." He was not able to foresee the encroaching development of Florida that is robbing the park of its lifeline of water. What is left of the Everglades must be saved—and that is the urgent message given by rangers and audiovisual presentations in the park. Because the Everglades is such a precious and unique resource, it was designated an International Biosphere Reserve in 1976 and a World Heritage Site in 1979 by the United Nations Educational, Scientific, and Cultural Organization (UNESCO).

A Park for the Birds

Much of the park's riches are not immediately apparent to the casual observer, but some are spectacular. We knew that few places anywhere offer a greater variety of beautiful and rare birds; about 300 species have been identified in the park.

But we hadn't realized how fascinating they would be. We watched an anhinga patiently hanging his wings out to dry, saw an osprey fly by with his fish lunch (to go) in his claws, and admired a bald eagle soaring above. For sheer beauty, we wonder if anything will ever top the pink blur that, as our boat drew near, turned out to be a flock of roseate spoonbills feeding.

Birds are the reason the Everglades is a national park, and a sad story it is. Until the Seminole Wars hardly anyone knew this wild area existed. But suddenly a new fashion craze brought unwanted attention. Plumed hats became de rigeur among the fashionable in society, and those plumes originated on two unfortunate species of egrets that lived in the Glades.

In the late 1800s and early 1900s hatmakers couldn't get enough of these lovely feathers. Before long they were paying a dollar a bird, good money in those days. Plume hunters, equipped with dugout canoes, guns, traps, and clubs, brutally slaughtered anything with feathers. They killed the adult birds while they nested, leaving new hatchlings to starve. This thirty-year massacre drove many species to the brink of extinction. Cypress Swamp, once swarming with more than two million wading birds, had only a few hundred thousand by the turn of the century.

Swimmer at Rest.
The anhinga is highly skilled at swimming and spear fishing. After impaling a fish on its pointed beak, the bird surfaces, flips its prey into the air, and swallows it head first. A golden-brown head and neck feathers distinguish the female anhinga from the male, whose plumage is greenish-black.

Day's End at Land's End.
The sun eases toward the Everglades horizon just as it has for eons. However, this unique and precious natural area has been drastically altered by an encroaching civilization. The glades will remain under seige as long as the development of Florida continues to tamper with its vital lifeline of water.

The Audubon Society, the first to try to save the birds, preached conservation before most of the world knew what the word meant. Unfortunately, Guy Bradley, the warden they hired to protect the egrets, was murdered by profit-hungry poachers. Undaunted, the society spearheaded a campaign to make plume hunting illegal and began the long struggle to turn the Everglades into a national park.

Everglades Wildlife

Of course, birds are but a part of the story. This mangrove wilderness, besides being one of the world's most unusual plant communities, is refuge for panther, crocodile, bobcat, deer, raccoon, diamondback terrapin, dolphin, and manatee, as well as a wide variety of fish.

The Everglades's subtropical climate governs its life. The nearly uniform warm, sunny weather makes the park a year-round attraction, but there are two distinct seasons. Winter is dry, and summer is very wet. Heavy rains fall during intense storms from May through October. Rainfall can exceed 50 inches a year. Warm, humid conditions bring out hordes of mosquitoes, sandflies, and other biting insects which are an important part of intricate food chains.

Crocodiles, much less common than alligators, are distinguished by their narrow snouts and greenish-gray color. The only crocodiles in the United States are found in southern Florida.

How the alligator got its name: Early Spanish settlers called this reptile "el lagarto," the lizard. Alligator is the corruption by English settlers of the Spanish name.

Alligators, once threatened by poachers, have made a comeback in recent years. Few residents of the Glades play a more vital role in the ecological balance of the area. In times of drought they move into deeper ponds and with powerful snout and tail thrashings root their way to the lowered water table. It is in these 'gator holes that the snails, fish, frogs, crustaceans, and turtles, as well as the larger creatures that feed on them, survive the dry season.

On our weekend afloat, we could feel ourselves gradually getting in tune with our surroundings and being lulled by the tranquility of the Glades. It was so still we could hear a dolphin breathe, and we loved listening for the beating of a whole skyful of wings as birds came in to roost at sundown. But if we were going to see the northern and western parts of the Glades, it was time to roll.

Northward to the Tamiami Trail and Shark Valley

We retraced our route from Flamingo to Homestead, drove north on SR 997 to the Tamiami Trail (US 41) and headed west across the lower tip of Florida. A number of compelling reasons made us stop, ranging from an airboat ride, which is not part of the park, to the tram ride at Shark Valley, which is. The air boat was exhilarating, if a little noisy, and Shark Valley was obviously a favorite refuge of birds and wild creatures. We were so intent on catching a glimpse of a rare wood stork, we practically stepped on an alligator!

We sampled Everglades frog legs and Indian fry bread in the Miccosukee Indian Restaurant, then toured the village of stilted chickees (huts) where some tribal members live as their ancestors did. Indians were doing beadwork, weaving baskets, and carving. We were not really enamored with the idea of the alligator wrestling exhibition, but enjoyed browsing in both the museum and gift shop. The Indians' struggle to hold on to their traditional ways is a grim reminder of a turbulent past. We learned the Miccosukees were not the first Indians to eke out a living from the Glades.

Everglades Indians—Past and Present

The Calusa Indians hunted and fished here nearly 2,000 years ago. Mound builders like the Indians of the middle west, the resourceful Calusas made saws from shark teeth, hammers from conch shells, and arrows with fire-hardened tips from sharpened reeds. Wary of invading Spaniards who made a practice of capturing Indians and making slaves of them, the Calusas attacked Ponce de León on his second voyage to the area.

The Indians were eventually annihilated by their contact with white men. Those not captured or killed succumbed to diseases introduced by the Europeans. By 1800 the only evidence left of the Calusas were great earthen mounds and huge piles of oyster shells.

During the first half of the nineteenth century American Indians migrated southward as white settlers invaded their hunting grounds. The official policy of the United States government was "Indian removal" to a

Nature's Cleanup Squad.
After a busy day, vultures settle down to roost for the night. An integral part of the complex ecology of the glades, these large birds eagerly consume carcasses of dead birds and animals.

place "far beyond the possibility of contact with white men." More than 4,000 Seminoles were forcibly taken from their Florida homeland and shipped to Oklahoma. Many died en route or shortly after arriving due to terrible living conditions. A few refused to leave, vowing to fight until death to defend their freedom.

During the Seminole Wars between 1835 and 1842, these defiant Indians were pushed into the Everglades. The farther into the wilderness they were driven, the more ferociously they fought. Though many were killed, the Seminoles resisted the United States government longer than any other North American tribe and was the only one never defeated.

Though fewer than 200 stood their ground deep in the Everglades, the Seminoles caused the army no end of grief. Efforts to subdue them cost more in casualties, lives, and money than any other battle against the Indians elsewhere in the country. More than a thousand men and $40 million were sacrificed for their unsavory cause. The Seminoles did not sign a peace treaty with the United States government until 1934.

The Indians lived in harmony with the Glades. Their diet consisted of turtle, deer, turkey, fish, shellfish, beans, squash, corn, cabbage palm, ibis, and coontie, a root that they grated and cooked. They traveled by canoe and lived in chickees, open platforms covered with thatched palm roofs.

The Miccosukee village we toured belongs to the descendants of these Indians. Although early white settlers referred to all the Florida Indians as Seminoles, two distinct tribes survive—the Miccosukees and the Cow

Indians made a "flour" for puddings from starch found in the coontie, a primitive plant related to pine and cypress. Poison was leached from the pounded pulp by straining it through a cloth.

Creek Seminoles. Each has a separate language the other tribe cannot understand.

Today they make their living cattle ranching, farming, fishing, and running attractions for tourists. The Miccosukees, true to the tradition of their ancestors, annually celebrate the harvest of the first roasting corn at their sacred Green Corn Dance. The astonishing thing is that all this goes on less than an hour's drive from the metropolis of Miami.

Driving in Panther Country

Urban development is a constant threat to yet another group of Everglades residents—the extremely endangered Florida panther. These big cats, also known as cougars, are among North America's rarest mammals. The remnant south Florida population—estimated to be only a few dozen—is all that remains of a great number of panthers that thrived in the eastern United States a hundred years ago.

Infrequent panther sightings have been reported in recent years on the stretch of road between Ochopee and SR 29, where we passed signs that read: "Panther Crossing—Next Five Miles." We kept a sharp eye out for one of these sleek gray cats even though chances of spotting one were, at best, slim.

We stumbled across America's smallest post office when we stopped in Ochopee to mail some postcards. Would the attendant mind if we took a photograph? Of course not. Like nearly all the folks we met in south Florida, she was friendly and eager to oblige. One obvious requirement of her job was that she be immune to claustrophobia. Her office is a tiny wooden structure measuring just seven by eight feet.

The Western Gateway of Everglades National Park

The Everglades, with its 1.4 million acres of varying environments, is not easy to sum up. At first, vast prairies of ten-foot-high sedge seemed to be the dominant feature, but we learned its intricate balance of life depends just as much on stands of pine and palmetto, freshwater sloughs, shallow offshore bays, and labyrinthine mangrove forests.

We were heading south on SR 29 toward Everglades City, the western gateway of the national park, where we planned to get acquainted with the Ten Thousand Islands area of the park. You don't travel very far down this road without realizing that the primary focus here is sportfishing, with boat tours running a close second.

Canoeing the Ten Thousand Islands

We decided to take the road less traveled and see what we could by canoe. The national park ranger strongly suggested going with an outfitter who knew the territory. Ten thousand, he told us, is an approximation, since new islands are constantly being formed, but it gives you some idea of the problem should you lose your way.

Our guide showed us how to use our paddles to dredge up oysters from the bottom and slurp them down for what were possibly the fresh-

Rural Delivery.
America's smallest post office can be found in Ochopee.

Sunset Cruise.
One can explore the country's largest subtropical wilderness in Everglades National Park.

est hors d'oeuvres we've ever had. That was just a warm-up for our gourmet dinner—sea trout flopped from the hook right into the frying pan. With appetites sharpened by exercise and salt air, we made quick work of our campfire supper.

High on the list of notorious Everglades wildlife are mosquitoes. We missed being able to retreat behind screens as we had on the houseboat. Days were no problem, but the early evening hours on the tiny island where we camped were spent huddling in the tent listening to frustrated

The Ten Thousand Islands in the Everglades are formed from bits of shell, driftwood, and seaweed that become trapped in the tangled roots of mangrove trees.

Happy Campers.
Happy campers are those who come
equipped with a bug-proof tent and
plenty of mosquito repellent. This
primitive campsite is on one of the
Ten Thousand Islands that pepper the
western section of Everglades
National Park.

mosquitoes that gave new meaning to the term bloodthirsty. Our guide
said this was nothing; we should see them in the summer. No thanks.

The very best part of canoeing is being able to get so close to so many
different kinds of birds. We will never forget the antics of pelicans dive-
bombing into the gulf in search of supper, herons making their dainty-
footed way along the shoreline, or the long graceful flight line of ibises
slicing the orange sun in half at day's end. We felt privileged to have had a
brief taste of this mysterious, ancient, water-and-land area we call the
Everglades.

POINTS OF INTEREST: Florida Tour 8

Biscayne and the Everglades

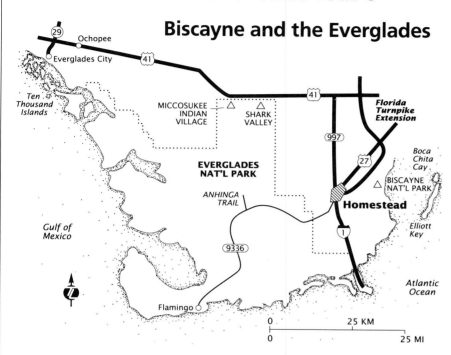

ACCESS: *Florida Turnpike Extension* to Tallahassee Road exit; follow signs to Biscayne National Park. Western gateway to the Everglades (Everglades City) may be reached from Naples via *I-75* and *SR 29*.

INFORMATION: *Biscayne National Park*, P.O. Box 1369, Homestead, FL 33090-1369 (305) 247-7275; *Everglades National Park*, Box 279, Homestead, FL 33030 (305) 247-6211; *Homestead Chamber of Commerce*, 650 US 1, Homestead, FL 33030 (305) 247-2332; *Everglades Area Chamber of Commerce*, P.O. Box E, Everglades City, FL 33929 (813) 695-3941.

ANNUAL EVENTS:

Homestead: *Frontier Days* (40-year-old festival features country musicians, dancing, steer wrestling, barrel races, cow-chip toss, old-fashioned barbecue), January/February; Homestead *Championship Rodeo*, February.

Everglades City: *Annual Everglades City Seafood Festival*, February.

Miami: *Miccosukee Indian Arts Festival* (tribal gathering, traditional dances, arts/crafts demonstrations), late December, early January.

SPECIAL ATTRACTIONS:

Homestead: *Orchid Jungle*, 26715 S.W. 157 Avenue, 33031 (305) 247-4824; *Fruit and Spice Park*, 24801 S.W. 187 Avenue, 33031 (305) 247-5727; *Miccosukee Indian Village & Cultural Center,* and *Airboat Rides* (includes museum and village of huts where tribal members live in traditional fashion) on US 41 (Tamiami Trail) approximately 25 miles west of Miami, P.O. Box 440021, Miami, FL 33144 (305) 223-8380.

BOAT TOURS AND OUTFITTERS:

Biscayne National Park: *Biscayne Aqua Center*, P.O. Box 1270, Homestead, FL 33030 (305) 247-2400.

Ten Thousand Islands area: *Everglades National Park Boat Tours*, P.O. Box 119, Everglades City, FL 33929 (813) 695-2591; *Port of the Islands*, Route 41, Naples, FL 33961 (813) 394-3101; *Captain Cecil Oglesby, Jr.*, P.O. Box 366, Chokoloskee, FL

33925 (813) 695-2910; *Everglades Canoe Outfitters*, 39801 Ingraham Highway, Homestead, FL 33040 (305) 246-1530; *Captain Bill Miller*, P.O. Box 306, Chokoloskee, FL 33925 (813) 695-4488; *Louis S. Daniels*, P.O. Box 284, Everglades City, FL 33929 (813) 695-2711; *Captain John Carlisle*, P.O. Box 27, Chokoloskee, FL 33925 (813) 695-3316; *Captain Don McKinnery*, P.O. Box 312, Chokoloskee, FL 33925 (813) 695-4950; *Captain Glenn Smallwood*, Everglades City, FL 33929 (813) 695-3531; *Captain Dennis Noble*, P.O. Box 62, Everglades City, FL 33929 (813) 695-2021.

Everglades Wilderness Waterway: Fully outfitted backcountry canoe trips, primarily during the winter months. *Everglades Canoe Outfitters*, 39801 Ingraham Highway, Homestead, FL 33040 (305) 246-1530; *Canoe Outpost Peace River*, c/o Jon Bragg, Route 7, Box 301, Arcadia, FL 33821 (813) 494-1215; *Mountain Workshop, Inc.*, c/o Corky Clark, P.O. Box 625, Ridgefield, CT 06877 (203) 438-3640; *North American Tours*, c/o David Harraden, 65 Black Point Road, Niantic, CT 06357 (203) 739-0791; *St. Regis Canoe Outfitters*, c/o David Cilley, P.O. Box 318, Lake Clear, NY 12945 (518) 891-1838; *Institute of Experiential Studies*, c/o Douglas Teschner, P.O. Box 23, Hadlyme, CT 06439 (203) 873-8658.

Everglades back country, Florida Bay, and the Gulf of Mexico. Boat tours and charter fishing trips, year-round: *Flamingo Lodge Marina and Outpost Resort* (houseboat rentals), P.O. Box 428, Flamingo, FL 33034 (305) 253-2241; *Shark Valley Tours* (tours along the Shark Valley loop road), P.O. Box 1729, Tamiami Station, Miami, FL 33144-1729 (305) 221-8455.

RESTAURANTS:

Miami area: *Miccosukee Indian Restaurant*, P.O. Box 440021, Miami, FL 33144, on US 41/Tamiami Trail approximately 25 miles west of Miami; (305) 223-8380 (Everglades cuisine; fry bread, catfish, Indian tacos, frog legs).

THE END OF THE ROAD
Miami to Key West

[Key West was] one of the most exhilarating experiences of my life; coming into Key West was like floating into a dream.

John dos Passos,
who rode a train into Key West in the 1920s

T he Keys were calling. They call every time winter gets the upper hand. We wanted to chase summertime to its year-round hangout and forget about snow. With dreams of tropical blossoms dancing in our heads, we started south on US 1. Since the trip from Miami to Key West can be made in about three hours driving straight through, it meant we could set an easy pace and make our leisurely way from island to island.

An Italian Renaissance Treasure

Typically, we hadn't even escaped the heavy traffic south of Miami before we found a compelling reason to stop on the bay side at 3251 South Miami Avenue in Coconut Grove. Villa Vizcaya is one of the grandest homes ever built in America, and its gardens have been called "the finest in the Western Hemisphere."

A dense stand of junglelike vegetation and stone fauns and nymphs guard the approach to this incredible mansion. Created by James Deering in 1916, Vizcaya epitomizes the glory of Italian Renaissance beautifully displayed in a seventy-room palazzo overlooking Biscayne Bay.

Deering, an International Harvester magnate, obviously had some spare pocket change as well as a grand vision of what he wanted for a winter hideaway. His search for the perfect location took him all over the world, but he claimed he could find no finer spot than the sunny shores of Biscayne Bay. Although sometimes as many as a thousand artisans were working at a time, completion of his dream home took five years—the result is magnificent.

As impressive as the house itself are the priceless treasures Deering had been collecting for twenty years before he began construction. Riches such as whole ceilings brought over from Italian Renaissance castles, a second-century Roman bath, ancient Persian rugs, and rare furniture from around the world seem perfectly at home here.

We strolled the elegant formal gardens admiring fountains, pools, classic statues, and meticulously trimmed jasmine hedges. This spectacular setting, we were told, undergoes dramatic change during an evening sound-and-light show, and at the annual Shakespeare Festival and Italian Renaissance Faire. (Call ahead for details, [305] 579-2808.)

Heading South for the Keys

US 1 between Miami and Homestead reflects the astonishing growth of Florida. Fast food outlets and tourist attractions competed for our attention, and we were relieved when the heavy traffic thinned out south of Homestead and Florida City. It was time to lose our mainland bonds and take to the sea.

Don't Go Near the Water.
Authoritative alligator is on duty at the "Danger Alligator" sign in Blue Hole, a rock quarry on Big Pine Key.

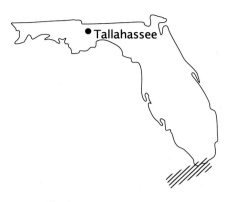

Tour **9** *157 miles*

VILLA VIZCAYA • OVERSEAS HIGHWAY • JOHN PENNEKAMP CORAL REEF STATE PARK • BAHIA HONDA STATE RECREATION AREA • NATIONAL KEY DEER REFUGE • KEY WEST • DRY TORTUGAS

Pretty Palazzo.
John Deering's Italian Renaissance palace,
Villa Vizcaya, is considered to be one of the
finest homes ever built in America.

National Geographic *called Vizcaya "a
triumph in recalling the Golden Age of
art and architecture . . . a repository of
Italian decorative art, unexcelled in
America." The home of the Dade County
Art Museum since 1952, the villa houses
a fine collection of fifteenth- to early
nineteenth-century European decorative arts as well as traveling art exhibits.*

From the signs beside the narrow two-lane road, it was obvious others
had been overly anxious to reach their destinations. The message, presented Burma-Shave style, warned: Patience—Pays—Only—5 Minutes—
To—Passing—Zone. Seems like a reasonable idea, especially for RVers.

Henry Flagler's Impossible Dream

The sunbaked Florida Keys are not going anywhere in a big hurry. These
subtropical islands of sand and palms are strung out like jewels on a
ribbon of concrete and steel (better known as the Overseas Highway).
This road has quite a history. Seems Henry Flagler had the brilliant idea of
linking this sleepy archipelago to the U.S. mainland by rail. The project
quickly became known as "Flagler's Folly," but this didn't faze the Standard Oil tycoon. "All you have to do," said the seventy-five-year-old
dreamer, "is to build one concrete arch, and then another, and pretty soon
you will find yourself in Key West."

Well, not exactly. Problems had a way of proliferating. In spite of intense heat, lack of water, mosquitoes, and hurricanes, Flagler never abandoned his original enthusiasm. He believed, as did many others, that Key West would become the American Gibraltar. The railroad, started in 1905, took seven years to build.

The gigantic undertaking was finally completed on January 21, 1912. The next day, when Flagler arrived aboard the first official train, Key West staged the largest celebration the island had ever seen. School children turned out to welcome the railroad's mastermind. Flagler walked on a thick carpet of roses gathered from local gardens to receive accolades from an excited citizenry. It was an emotional moment for the eighty-three-year-old visionary whose last great dream had finally become reality. His life's work completed, Flagler was to die the following year.

Despite early rave reviews, the railroad proved to be an economic disaster. Cargoes fell well below optimistic projections, and too few wealthy visitors could be lured so far from the mainland. The Great Depression dealt a lethal blow to the staggering enterprise, but it was violent weather that finally finished it off.

The worst hurricane the area had ever known devastated the Keys on Labor Day in 1935. A twenty-foot wall of water smashed the islands, and the barometer registered 26.35, the lowest reading ever recorded in the Western Hemisphere. The storm swept a train into the sea and washed away many miles of track along with most of the embankments. The death toll, estimated at about 500 people, also included one railroad, a magnificent achievement whose moment in the sun was over.

After the severing of their railroad umbilical cord, the Keys experienced 2½ years of relative isolation. Fortunately, the state of Florida acquired property rights and began building a modern highway on the old railroad bed. The 128-mile Overseas Highway, completed in 1938, was the first rung on the area's desperately needed economic-recovery ladder.

We were pleased to be able to enjoy the fruits of all these past labors. You don't drive very far along this highway without appreciating what an amazing engineering feat it is. In the early 1980s thirty-seven bridges were replaced with wider, heavier spans, including the famous Seven-Mile Bridge between Marathon and Duck Key, the longest and largest span on the Overseas Highway. This modernization has made travel much easier and safer for the RVer. We remember the days when you had to hold your breath when you passed another rig on a bridge. The improved highway is also a boon to the local populace, who depend heavily on tourism for their livelihood.

Since there is only one road to Key West, we weren't in any danger of getting lost; keeping track of our progress was a cinch. Small, green mile markers on the right side of the road begin with number 126 a mile past Florida City on US 1 and end with a zero mile marker in Key West. These markers, used instead of addresses, make it easy to locate places. (A restaurant named Marker 88 not only serves great food but is obviously a snap to find.)

Highway to the Sea.
The 128-mile Overseas Highway (US 1), which connects the Florida Keys with the U.S. mainland, provides motorists with the most spectacular over-water drive in the world. The highway consists of 113 miles of roadway and 42 bridges, including the country's longest continuous span—the Seven-Mile Bridge.

Sometimes as many as 4,000 laborers at a time (many were skid row bums imported from northern cities) worked on the railroad to Key West. The total cost of the project came to 700 lives and approximately $50 million.

Key Largo—Gateway to the Conch Republic

A barrage of signs on Key Largo greeted us. One billboard stood out: "The Conch Republic Welcomes You." Talk about bravado! This friendly, free wheeling community once seceded from the Union, established the Conch Republic, and demanded foreign aid from the U.S. government!

Natives are called Conchs (pronounced "konks") after the mollusk that thrives in local waters, but transients abound. When we asked one waiter how long he'd been in the Keys, he checked his watch (for the time, not the date) before replying. All agree the attitude here *is* different. These mellow folks measure time by watching the sun rise over the Atlantic then strolling to the other side of the island to watch it slide into the Gulf of Mexico.

Underwater at Pennekamp State Park

The Upper Keys, those nearest the mainland, offer every type of watery pleasure ranging from diving (there are more dive shops per mile in the Keys than anywhere else in the world), parasailing, and windsurfing to sunset cruises. Views of ocean and gulf are spectacular, but to us the most

By the Beautiful Sea.
Although John Pennekamp State Park on Key Largo is known primarily as a magnificent underwater preserve, its topside view is also noteworthy. Outstanding campgrounds, nature trails, and beaches offer RVers a very special place in the sun.

remarkable scenery lies below the surface in John Pennekamp Coral Reef State Park. Although there were plenty of signs welcoming RVers on Key Largo, we chose Pennekamp for our first few nights in the Keys. Previous experience had taught us to make reservations well ahead at this popular tourist site.

John Pennekamp State Park, the nation's first underwater park, protects about 180 square miles of rainbow-colored coral gardens and exotic tropical fish on the only living reef along the Atlantic Coast. Severely damaged by commercial souvenir hunters who ripped into it with dynamite and crowbars in the 1930s and 1940s, the reef has recovered beautifully thanks to a conservation movement led by the late John Pennekamp, an associate editor of the *Miami Herald*.

For a close-up look beneath the Atlantic, the park offers everything from snorkeling tours and glass-bottom-boat trips to scuba diving. Rental canoes, runabouts, sea kayaks, and windsurfers are also available. Besides having a lovely place to camp, we had access to the full-service dive shop, a couple of nature trails, and several sandy beaches at this twenty-one-mile-long park.

Three days and two sunburns later, we were on the road again recounting the wonders of Pennekamp. We had seen unbelievable neon-colored fish, fantastic coral formations, and a nine-foot bronze underwater statue, *Christ of the Deep*. More fun than the rough-water glass-bottom-boat tour (take your Dramamine!) was the time we spent snorkeling. Clearwater views to sixty feet gave us a window on a world of exquisite beauty we won't soon forget.

Through the Middle and Lower Keys

The waterscapes on both sides of US 1 seemed to blossom and expand as we drove south. Pines, palms, and mangroves framed ocean views that shifted from turquoise and violet to milky emerald and navy blue. But the Key's riches are not only to be found in its scenery.

The Middle and Lower Keys from Long Key to Key West are rife with stories of shipwrecks and fabulous buried treasure. Once, Spanish ships laden with riches from Central America were routinely plundered as they passed these islands. Such famous pirates as Black Caesar, Blackbeard, and Lafitte found the many inlets and coves of the Keys ideal for concealing their ships and stashing their booty. Today, from time to time a lucky beachcomber uncovers a genuine gold doubloon.

Bahia Honda State Recreation Area

We stopped just before the Seven-Mile Bridge in Marathon for a chili dog with cheese and a slice of Key lime pie at the Seven Mile Grill. After crossing this engineering marvel (the country's longest continuous bridge boasting the highest point—sixty-five feet—in the Keys), we turned into Bahia Honda State Recreation Area. The palm-shaded beach here gets our vote as the most beautiful in the Keys.

Remember the movie Key Largo *with Humphrey Bogart, Lauren Bacall, and Edward G. Robinson caught in the grip of a brutal hurricane? The walls of the Caribbean Club Bar at Mile Marker 104, supposedly the setting for a small part of the film, are plastered with movie photos.*

Down to the Sea in Ships (and RVs). The Florida Keys are sometimes called "the land that's mostly water." If you're not gazing at the Atlantic Ocean, Florida Bay, or the Gulf of Mexico, you're probably overlooking a lagoon or canal.

Down among the Sheltering Palms.
This idyllic, palm-shaded beach at Bahia Honda State Recreation Area resembles a tropical island in the South Pacific. Two campgrounds—one fairly open near the marina and west swimming area, the other shady and more secluded—tempt RVers to linger.

Bahia Honda is the bony skeleton of an ancient coral reef covered by beach, dunes, coastal strand hammocks, and mangroves. At the far end of Sandspur Beach, a nature trail follows the shore of a tidal lagoon, then winds through a coastal strand hammock, and returns to the beach.

This southernmost state recreation area is the perfect place to while away the hours beachcombing, swimming, fishing, exploring, and bird watching. Some of the unusual growth on this botanically unique spit of land—satinwood trees, spiny catesbaeas and dwarf morning glories—were carried from the West Indies by way of waves, winds, and birds. The white-crowned pigeon, great white heron, roseate spoonbill, reddish egret, osprey, brown pelican, and least tern are but a few of the rare and beautiful birds that use the island as a way station.

We climbed the old Bahia Honda Bridge for a glorious view of the area, which includes the original Flagler train trestle and the abandoned narrow span where more than one RV lost an outside mirror in a highway squeeze play. Many of the old bridges in the Upper and Lower Keys, including this one, offer anglers spots to dangle their hooks for mackerel, bluefish, tarpon, snook, grouper, and jewfish. According to a park ranger, tarpon fishing in Bahia Honda (Spanish for "deep bay") rates among the best in the country.

Small Deer on Big Pine Key

The end of the road beckoned, but we had definitely been affected by the clock in the Seven Mile Grill, which instead of displaying numbers posed the philosophical question, "Who cares?" In Big Pine Key, we stopped at the tiny chamber of commerce building for tips on the best spots to see Key deer.

We found a few dainty deer about the size of large dogs wandering among the pines in the National Wildlife Refuge for Key Deer just north of US 1. These descendants of the Virginia white-tailed deer range over more than a dozen neighboring islands, but about 250 of the estimated 400 Key deer live on Big Pine. This, by the way, is also the home of old pineapple plantations and the state's only primeval stand of tree cacti.

Key West—The End of the Road

Our reward at the end of the Overseas Highway was Key West, a three-by-five-mile island where Hemingway wrote his novels, John James Audubon painted tropical birds, and Mel Fisher dredged up a stupendous fortune diving for sunken treasure. Spaces for RVs are limited on this small island (especially in February) so we had written ahead for reservations at Boyd's, which bills itself as the "southernmost campground in the U.S.A. on the ocean."

The campground is actually on Stock Island, the last island before Key West. Public bus service is available a half block from Boyd's, which we recommend using. We saw a few motorhomes navigating in the congested Mallory Square area, but they were having a rough time. The RV is handy for visiting outlying sights or for parking beside the public beach. But for downtown sightseeing, Key West is best approached on foot, by bike, or on rented motorscooter. A good way to get an overview of the island is to hop aboard the Conch Tour Train (an open-air tram) or join an Old Town Trolley tour, which leaves from Mallory Square or can be joined via the trolley that tours the island.

On the trolley we learned Key West has had more than its share of ups and downs. In the 1830s it enjoyed prosperity thanks to its chief industry—salvaging, or wrecking. Strong currents and tides, reefs, hurricanes, and a lack of lighthouses made shipwrecks the order of the day. In 1825 Congress passed legislation requiring that all salvage from wrecks in U.S. waters be taken to an American port for arbitration.

Invading tribes from the north cornered the Calusa Indians on the island of Key West where they made their final, unsuccessful stand. The Spanish explorers, who came upon the grisly remains of the battle, named the island Cayo Hueso, which means island of bones. Eventually, this was Anglicized into Key West.

Located 90 miles north of Havana, 159 miles south of Miami, and 65 miles west of all of South America, Key West is the southernmost city in the continental United States.

La Concha, Key West's first and only high-rise downtown hotel, cost a whopping $898,000 in 1925. Harry Truman was a guest, Ernest Hemingway mentioned the hotel in his famous Key West novel, To Have and Have Not, *and Tennessee Williams completed the final draft of* A Streetcar Named Desire *here.*

The Write Place.
Ernest Hemingway loved his Spanish-Colonial home in Key West, where he wrote some of his most famous novels.

"They live by it," wrote a visitor about Key West residents in 1855, adding that "it is the first thing at sunrise and the last thing at sunset for them to look out for a wreck." No wonder. The first crew to reach the foundering ship could claim the entire cargo. Bad luck for some meant good luck for others. Key West, a natural center for the auction of cargoes and repair of ships, quickly became the wealthiest city per capita in the entire country.

Wrecking fortunes went to work building splendid houses—one more grand than the next. We found some heavily gingerbreaded masterpieces that had recently been restored to their former glory. It wasn't hard to imagine long, leisurely afternoons spent sipping rum punches on those wide porches. The architecture, a fascinating blend of Bahamian, Spanish, New England, and Southern styles, includes "conch" houses constructed in the Bahamas and shipped on schooners to Key West. The chamber of commerce at Mallory Square provided a handy "Pelican Path" folder, a walking guide to old homes, which are mostly located between Carolina, Angel, Duval, and Francis streets.

Walking does whet the appetite. Luckily, Key West food is really special. The emphasis is on fresh as in catch-of-the-day and tropical fruits right off the tree. This is the place to enjoy stone crabs, raw conch salad, Key lime pie (green imitations don't count; the real thing, made from the Key limes that grow only in these islands, is more yellow), and bollos (hush puppies made from mashed black-eyed peas instead of corn meal).

Our idea of a perfect lunch is a cup of black bean soup, conch fritters, and peel-your-own shrimp in the open-air "Grog and Oyster Bar" in the beautifully restored Hotel La Concha. For dinner, it's hard to beat Florida lobster under the stars at Louie's Backyard.

How could we pass up the Ernest Hemingway home? After all, it was here that "Papa" wrote some of his best books including *A Farewell to Arms* and *For Whom the Bell Tolls*. His home, an imposing Spanish-colonial-style mansion, was built in 1851 and purchased by the author in 1931. Descendants of his six-toed cats roam the yard, which is overgrown with exotic plants and trees. After writing all morning and fishing all afternoon, the author would stop at Sloppy Joe's (where we later found more Hemingway memorabilia) for some local chitchat and a Scotch-on-the-rocks.

We also paid our respects to John James Audubon by visiting the house where he spent some time in 1832 studying and sketching tropical birds. Furnished with eighteenth- and nineteenth-century antiques, the restored house contains the naturalist-artist's original engravings and a video of Florida birds from Audubon's *Birds of America*.

Within easy walking distance we found a complete change of pace at the movie, *The Key West Picture Show*. If you want to meet some of Key West's more unconventional residents, enjoy satire, and have a quirky sense of humor, this definitely should not be missed.

Mel Fisher spent sixteen years searching for the *Atocha*, one of two Spanish galleons that went down in a hurricane off Key West on September 20, 1622. In his case persistence paid off on July 20, 1985, to the tune of $400 million in gold, silver, and emeralds. Of course, we would go see the Mel Fisher Maritime Heritage Society Museum where the great treasures from both the *Atocha* and the *Santa Margarita* are displayed.

A Seaplane Adventure to Fort Jefferson

Enough of vicarious living: The sea was full of riches; we wanted to don our snorkels and explore. Electric-blue and yellow fish swimming in and out of elkhorn coral—now there's a treasure! Snorkeling off Fort Jefferson in the Dry Tortugas promised to be a treat, but there is more to this adventure than parrot fish and gracefully waving sea fans.

After laboring through the water for a short way, our six-seater seaplane finally took off from Stock Island, made a steep turn, and headed for the Tortugas. "Look out here on my side," the pilot said. "A shark, and is he ever a whopper." Sure enough, a streamlined shark was idly cruising through the crystalline water below. Soon we were passing over an idyllic circle of islands known as the Marqueses, a small submerged plane (a drug deal gone sour), and the site of the *Atocha* shipwreck where treasure hunter Mel Fisher hit pay dirt.

Sixty-eight miles and thirty-five minutes later, our low-flying craft reached Fort Jefferson, a sprawling rosy fortress surrounded on all six sides by powder-blue water. This impressive structure with its fifty-foot walls and water-filled moat had an enthusiastic welcoming committee in the form of one very friendly egret. The pilot explained that sometimes birds get blown in by a storm and have to depend on handouts. So, it was our lunch he was after!

Birdman of Key West.
John J. Audubon, famed naturalist and artist, stayed in this gracious home in 1832 while studying the fascinating birdlife of the Florida Keys. Authentically restored and furnished with period antiques, the Audubon House is now a museum.

Gibraltar of the Gulf.
Fort Jefferson National Monument includes a sprawling six-sided fort, largest of the nineteenth-century American coastal forts, and seven islands (Dry Tortugas), inhabited by tropical ocean birds.

Shrimp Boats Are a-Coming.
Residents of the Florida Keys have long looked to the sea for inspiration as well as sustenance. The setting sun provides a daily cause for celebration at Mallory Docks in Key West, the southernmost city in the continental United States.

In an orientation slide program we learned that construction on Fort Jefferson, which began in 1846, was never completed. Considered obsolete because of the invention of the rifled cannon, the fort was used primarily as a prison for deserters during the Civil War. In 1865, the four "Lincoln Conspirators," condemned for their part in the assassination of Abraham Lincoln, were imprisoned here, including Dr. Samuel Mudd, the physician who set John Wilkes Booth's broken leg after Booth shot Lincoln. Mudd earned an early pardon by administering to victims of a yellow-fever epidemic that swept through the fort. What gave me a thrill was knowing that my great-grandfather had served as a medic at Fort Jefferson during the Civil War.

A Farewell Party for the Sun

We arrived back in Key West in plenty of time to catch the sunset at Mallory Docks. If you want to mingle with a weird crowd in a carnival atmosphere, this is definitely the place to be. The end of the road attracts an astonishing variety of people, from Key West's large gay community to tourists of all ages. One man shows off his pet iguana, another swallows a series of flaming swords, but the main attraction is always the sun making its slow but purposeful way toward the ocean. A dazzling performance never fails to get a standing ovation!

POINTS OF INTEREST: Florida Tour 9

Miami to Key West

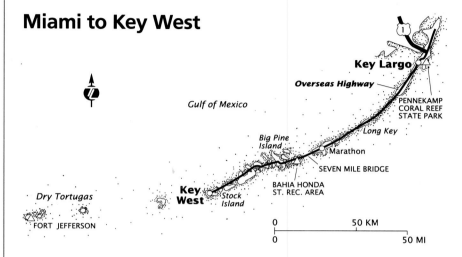

ACCESS: *I-95 south to US 1.*

INFORMATION: *Florida Keys Visitors Bureau*, P.O. Box 1147, Key West, Florida Keys 33041-1147 (800) FLA-KEYS or (305) 296-3811; *Key West Chamber of Commerce*, Key West, FL 33041 (305) 294-2587; *Lower Keys Chamber of Commerce*, Big Pine Key, FL 33043 (305) 872-2411; *Key Largo Chamber of Commerce*, Key Largo, FL 33037 (305) 451-1414; *The Greater Miami Convention & Visitors Bureau*, 4770 Biscayne Blvd., Miami, FL 33137 (305) 573-4300.

ANNUAL EVENTS:

Miami: *Italian Renaissance Festival*, Vizcaya Museum and Gardens, March.

Key West: *Buskerfest* (five days of musicians, mimes, jugglers, fire-eaters, and other street performers), *Days of the Civil War, Key West Literary Seminar*, January; *Old Island Days* (house and garden tours), January–March; *Witness the Massing of the Colours* (honoring those who served our country), February; *Conch Republic Celebration* (fishing tournament, Battle of the Tall Ships), April.

MUSEUMS AND GALLERIES:

Miami: *Vizcaya Museum and Gardens*, 3251 S. Miami Avenue, Miami, FL 33137 (305) 579-2813.

Key West: *Hemingway House and Museum*, 907 Whitehead St., Key West, FL 33040 (305) 294-1575; *Audubon House and Gardens*, 205 Whitehead St., Key West, FL 33040 (305) 294-2116; *Mel Fisher Maritime Heritage Society Museum*, 200 Greene Street, Key West, FL 33040 (305) 296-9936.

SPECIAL ATTRACTIONS:

Key Largo: *John Pennekamp Coral Reef State Park*, P.O. Box 487, Key Largo, FL 33037 (305) 451-1202.

Homestead: *Fort Jefferson National Monument* (68 miles west of Key West, reached by boat or seaplane), P.O. Box 279, Homestead, FL 33030 (305) 247-6211. For transportation, contact Key West Chamber of Commerce (see above).

OUTFITTERS:

Coral Reef Park Company (sailing, canoeing, scuba diving, windsurfing, kayaking, snorkeling, glass-bottom-boat tours at John Pennekamp Coral Reef State Park), P.O. Box 1560, Key Largo, FL 33037 (305) 451-1621.

Club Nautico of Key West, (deep-sea fishing, sailing, or diving), 711 Eisenhower Dr., Key West, FL 33040 (305) 294-2225.

Captain Nemo's Glass Bottom Boat Tours, Galleon Marina, Key West, FL 33040 (305) 294-8856.

Captain Franco Piacibello, (snorkeling and scuba-diving trips), Reef Raiders Dive Shop, 109 Duval St., Key West, FL 33040 (305) 294-3635.

RESTAURANTS:

Key West: *Oyster Bar, Holiday Inn La Concha*, 430 Duval Street, Key West, FL 33040 (305) 296-2991 (fresh seafood, raw bar, specialty drinks; 50s atmosphere); *Louie's Backyard*, 700 Waddell, Key West (305) 294-1061 (fresh seafood and other local favorites, oceanfront outdoor dining).

Index

Page numbers in **boldface** refer to illustrations in the text.